IMAGES
of Sport

BRADFORD
RUGBY LEAGUE CLUB

BRADFORD, NORTHERN AND BULLS

Eric Batten was a dashing, free-scoring right winger. He played in 5 Challenge Cup finals for Bradford (in 1944-45 and 1947-49), was a British Lion in 1946 and won most of the game's major honours. This classic image shows Eric making his trademark leap over a Leeds opponent at Headingley in 1947.

IMAGES
of Sport

BRADFORD
RUGBY LEAGUE CLUB
BRADFORD, NORTHERN AND BULLS

Compiled by
Robert Gate

TEMPUS

First Published 2000
Reprinted 2002
Copyright © Robert Gate, 2000

Tempus Publishing Limited
The Mill, Brimscombe Port,
Stroud, Gloucestershire, GL5 2QG

ISBN 0 7524 1896 3

Typesetting and origination by
Tempus Publishing Limited
Printed in Great Britain by
Midway Colour Print, Wiltshire

Also available from Tempus Publishing

Castleford RLFC	David Smart	0 7524 1895 5
Halifax RLFC	Andrew Hardcastle	0 7524 1831 9
Headingley RLFC Voices	Phil Caplan	0 7524 1822 X
Hunslet RLFC	Les Hoole	0 7524 1641 3
Leeds RLFC	Phil Caplan & Les Hoole	0 7524 1140 3
Salford RLFC	Graham Morris	0 7524 1897 1
Sheffield Eagles RLFC	John Cornwell	0 7524 1830 0
St Helens RLFC	Alex Service	0 7524 1883 1
Warrington RLFC	Gary Slater & Eddie Fuller	0 7524 1870 X
Yorkshire Rugby League	Les Hoole	0 7524 1881 5
Five Nations	David Hands	0 7524 1851 3
Burnley FC: 1882-1968	Ray Simpson	0 7524 1520 4
Bury FC: 1882-1968	Peter Cullen	0 7524 1526 3
Leeds United FC	David Saffer	0 7524 1642 1
Rotherham United FC	Gerry Somerton	0 7524 1670 7
Sheffield United FC	Denis Clarebrough	0 7524 1059 8
York City FC	David Batters	0 7524 1568 9
Yorkshire CCC	Mick Pope	0 7524 0756 2

Contents

Robbie Paul, an Odsal icon. One of the modern greats, Robbie Paul has been a central figure at Bradford from the club's last days as Northern in 1994/95 into the Super League era of Bull mania.

Introduction

The completion of this book was unavoidably delayed, but for the best possible reason. Bradford Bulls had reached the Challenge Cup final and it would have been inconceivable to release the book without reference to the momentous event at Murrayfield on 29 April 2000.

Bradford beat Leeds in an absorbing final and brought the Challenge Cup back to the city after an absence of fifty-one long years. This bald statistic of over half a century between Challenge Cup triumphs is in fact an accurate reflection of the club's entire history. For a club in a city the size of Bradford, real success has been relatively rare. Of course, there have been periods of greatness, stretching right back into the 1880s when the club was a member of the Rugby Football Union. In the very early days of the Northern Union the club, still known simply as Bradford, was a real power and there are many people who still recall the glorious roaring '40s and even more who recall with pride and pleasure the double champions of 1979/80 and 1980/81. The last few years of the twentieth century brought a renaissance at Odsal with Wembley appearances in 1996 and 1997 and the Super League title in 1997. The Murrayfield triumph may well be the prelude to another purple patch for the club.

However, for every success the club has enjoyed it has endured long and sometimes traumatic periods of failure. The cycle of booms and busts has been more marked at Bradford than at most clubs and those who run the club should heed the lessons of history. Both the cataclysmic events of 1907 and 1963, the seemingly endless years of penury and dismal results, followed in the wake of apparently never-ending halcyon days.

Bradford's history as a rugby club began in 1863 and is one of the longest and most interesting in Yorkshire. Their first games were played at Horton cricket ground on All Saints Road and after several migrations the club settled at Park Avenue in 1880. In 1907 they were expelled to make way for the newly formed soccer club Bradford Park Avenue, despite the fact that they had been one of the most prominent rugby (RU and NU) clubs in history. The 1907/08 season saw them housed at Greenfield Athletic Ground, Dudley Hill, and a year later they moved to the infamously inadequate Birch Lane. The club finally came to rest at Odsal in 1934, where its supporters still patiently wait for the monumental developments which have been promised for the last sixty-odd years – though perhaps now with real hope.

Down the years the team have been known, amongst other things, as the Park Avenuites, the Steam Pigs, the Odsalites, Northern and latterly the Bulls. Nowadays they style themselves, much to the annoyance of almost everyone outside Bradford, as the 'People's Team'. The irony is that Bradford developed from a socially elite club back in Victorian times when Manningham were more entitled to call themselves Bradfordians' 'People's Team'. Bradford were so superior in those days that they refused to play Wakefield Trinity, who were too intent on winning. For a period in the 1880s they also refused to take part in the Yorkshire Cup, which the Yorkshire proletariat were obsessed with.

The sobriquet of the People's Team may well serve as a rallying call for today's club and supporters, but the long view of Bradford's premier rugby club, in its guises as Bradford, Northern and the Bulls, would indicate that a more appropriate epithet would be the 'Curate's Egg' club.

The most interesting Rugby League club histories are those which mingle triumph with disaster. Bradford's history is replete with both.

Robert Gate
Ripponden
May 2000

Acknowledgements

Many people have given help in the compilation of this book. Several have been absolutely invaluable in providing images and information. Chief amongst these have been Andy Howard, Andrew Cudbertson, Trevor Delaney, Timothy Auty, Tony Collins and my brother, Charles Gate. Andy Howard has provided the vast majority of the modern photographs, including the shots of the Murrayfield triumph which were required at the last moment, while Andrew Cudbertson has furnished the book with many of the 1980s images. Trevor Delaney, Timothy Auty and the RFL's archivist, Tony Collins, kindly assisted with quantities of the older material.

Others who have contributed images or assistance are, in no particular order: Harry Edgar (*Open Rugby*), *The Rugby Leaguer*, *The Bradford Telegraph & Argus* and its predecessors, *The Yorkshire Post*, John Oakes (Micron Video), John Huxley, Mike Gardner, Piers Morgan and the RFU, Roger Shackleton, Henry Skrzpiecki, Curtis Johnstone, Alex Service, Alex Majidi, John and Brenda Graves, Andy Cole and Brian Walker. Thanks also to those anonymous photographers, artists, cartoonists and writers of long ago whose work has so fortuitously survived to enrich this work. If any copyrights have been infringed, there has been no intent and if anyone who has helped has been omitted from the acknowledgements, the fault is the author's whose memory must have failed him.

Pre-Pokemon – an Edwardian Baines card depicting young Bradford supporters trading Northern Union cards.

One
Before the
Northern Union
1864-1895

An 1880s Baines card. This coloured relic depicts the Bradford player in the club's ancient livery of red, amber and black.

F. S. TETLEY.
*(From a Photograph by Appleton & Co.,
Bradford.)*

The first Bradford player to win an international cap was Tom Tetley, who played in the three-quarters for England against Scotland at The Oval in 1876. This was the last international match to be played with twenty players a side. Tetley was a noted athlete, winning many 100-yard races. As a rugby player he was reputed to have a powerful hand-off and was the devil to tackle.

The humour in this cartoon from December 1884 may be a little lost on twenty-first century observers. It does, however, accurately reflect the social interactions and tensions that were invading rugby in late Victorian times. As a socially elite club, Bradford placed great value on playing sides such as Oxford University, Cambridge University, Blackheath, Fettes-Loretto and Lansdowne. Many of their supporters, however, came from a class who did not give a damn and whose priorities were a team that won and a game which entertained.

A NEW PLAYER.
Little Aitchless, *a Bradford limb of the law, goes to the Bradford v. Oxford University Football Match, and, hearing all the partisans of the University shouting* "'Varsity, 'Varsity," *asks another limb of the law*: "I say, old fellow, which of the players is the fellow called "Varsity'? Seems to be a big favourite anyhow."

Harry Wharfedale Tennant Garnett was one of the major figures in Victorian rugby. He captained Bradford from 1874 to 1881 and led Yorkshire from 1877 to 1880. As a forward, he had weight and was a fine dribbler and kicker, who won an England cap against the Scots in 1877. Garnett refused to wear stockings or shin-pads 'having whilst a schoolboy learnt to despise a hack'. He was the first president of the Yorkshire Rugby Union, from 1876 to 1883, and president of the Rugby Football Union from 1889 to 1890.

Aubrey B. Perkins was so highly regarded by his fellow players and officials that he was nicknamed 'Able Bodied' Perkins. His rugby career began as a half-back with Bradford Caledonians and he continued in that position with Bradford when they played at Apperley. After the move to Park Avenue he joined the pack and won a Yorkshire cap against Cheshire in 1883. He was elected Bradford captain for the 1882/83 season. In 1890/91 he was elected Yorkshire's senior vice-president. He was also a prominent bicyclist.

Joe Hawcridge was the Robbie Paul of the 1880s. Known as the 'Artful Dodger', a nickname bestowed on many a clever player in this period, he was the idol of Park Avenue crowds. A former Manningham player, he won 2 England caps in 1885 – a poor return and clear evidence of southern bias, according to his admirers. His elusiveness and speed were regarded as extraordinary, bringing him 38 tries in a single season, an astronomical total for the times. He kept a hatter's shop in Bradford but later emigrated to USA where he died in 1905.

The Robertshaw brothers were a major force within the Bradford club during the 1880s. From left to right are Rawson, Percy and Herbert. A fourth, Jere, also played. Rawson Robertshaw is credited with perfecting the art of English centre play and was dubbed 'the Prince of Centres' thirty years before Huddersfield's Harold Wagstaff was accorded a similar title. Rawson won 5 England caps between 1886 and 1887. Percy, a full-back, also won an England cap in 1888. Herbert was considered the most brilliant Bradford forward of his era. Amazingly, all four brothers won Yorkshire caps.

This splendidly evocative cartoon depicts the Manchester versus Bradford match of 8 November 1884. It was published in the bizarrely titled Bradford weekly magazine, *Toby, The Yorkshire Tyke*. 'Joa' in the central image is undoubtedly Joe Hawcridge, making another of his sensational runs. Like Bradford, Manchester were regarded as a socially elite club.

13

In 1884 Bradford won the Yorkshire Cup for the only time in its existence as a Rugby Union club. On the way to the final, Bradford despatched Stanley, Wakefield St Austin's, Manningham, Ossett and Batley. From left to right, back row: H. Robertshaw, Asquith. Middle row: Carter, Perkins, Bottomley, Ritchie, Atkinson, Richmond, Booth, Barker, Wright, Critchley, Haigh. Front row: R. Bonsor, Marshall, Hickson, F. Bonsor, Wilkinson, R. Robertshaw, Potter.

The final at Cardigan Fields, Leeds, saw Bradford demolish Hull by a goal and four tries to a solitary try – a huge margin by the standards of the day. In the absence of action photography, artists' impressions of incidents had to enliven reports of the game. Here, Herbert Rawson is shown about to score the last try.

One of the great heroes of Bradford and Yorkshire rugby in this period was Fred Bonsor, captain of the Yorkshire Cup winning XV and a try-scorer in the final. Bonsor was regarded as the best half-back that Yorkshire had produced and became the first Yorkshireman to captain England when he led them to victory over the New Zealand Natives in 1889. However, in 1890 he chose to play for Bradford against Dewsbury in a Yorkshire Cup-tie instead of for England against Scotland and was never selected again. Bonsor was awarded the DCM in the Boer War.

In November 1884 Bradford annoyed the Yorkshire Union by refusing to allow several players to play in the Roses Match at Manchester. Instead, they played for the club at Blackheath. A massive victory ensued for Bradford, who had wanted their best men available as Blackheath were notorious for bringing in ringers for important games. This cartoon pointedly ridicules Blackheath's duplicity by referring to them as Marlborough Nomads, another genuine club which played at Blackheath but who were not really in the same class.

By the 1880s dozens of rugby clubs had sprung up in the Bradford area, all anxious to join the ranks of the elite. A thriving trade also burgeoned in football cards, particularly those manufactured by John Baines of 15 North Parade, Bradford. Baines became a wealthy man and other manufacturers copied his success. Many local teams were commemmorated on these cards, which are nowadays collectors' items. Shipley were amongst the most successful of Bradford's junior clubs and won the Bradford Charity Cup in 1888/89. This card shows Herbert Ward, who later played for Bradford in the Northern Union after winning an England Rugby Union cap in 1895 against Wales.

Bowling were a thriving club by 1882, when their headquarters and dressing rooms were at the Greenfield Hotel, Dudley Hill. At that time their club colours were described as 'navy blue with a white Maltese cross'. This card, however, probably dates from the 1890s as it is scarlet and white, the club colours of this later period.

In 1882 Bowling had strong local opposition in the Dudley Hill club which hitherto had been known as Bierley. Their base and ground were at the White Hart Inn, Rooley Lane. They also played in navy blue but with a solitary white band.

J. CAMPBELL, CAPT.
PLAY UP "SALTAIRE."

Saltaire's ground was at Albert Road, two minutes walk from Saltaire Station, while they used Saltaire Baths as dressing rooms. This card probably dates from around 1885, when the club's colours were navy blue and gold.

BRADFORD'S FOOTBALL FIVE.

(From Photographs by Messrs. BROWN, BARNES & BELL, *of Kirkgate, Bradford, and Commercial Street, Leeds.)*

F. T. RITCHIE.

J. W. MARSHALL.

F. BONSOR *(Captain)*.

J. L. HICKSON.

S. ASQUITH.

To which are added some reminiscences of last Saturday's match.

This celebration of Bradford's players and some of their keener or more devious supporters is a graphic illustration of the hold the game had on the district in the 1880s. All 'Bradford's Football Five' were local heroes who had represented Yorkshire.

Laurie Hickson was another highly influential figure in Bradford and Yorkshire rugby. A forceful forward and unusually prolific as a try-scorer for the time, Hickson joined Bradford from Bingley in 1881 and was capped 28 times by Yorkshire between 1883 and 1890, attaining the captaincy in 1889. He was also capped 7 times by England. From 1913 to his death in 1920 he was president of the Yorkshire RFU. During the Great War he was a prime mover in the formation of the Bradford Athletic Batallion.

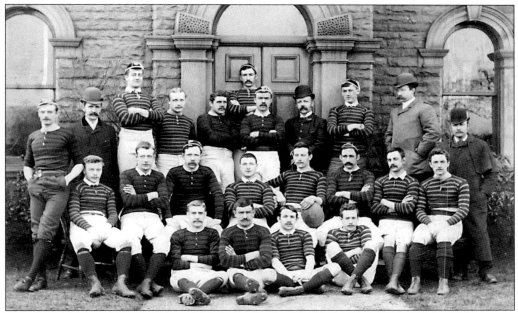

Bradford, *c.* 1888. Six England internationals can be seen among the players – Fred Bonsor (extreme left, hands in pockets), Laurie Hickson (third left, standing with arms folded), Herbert Robertshaw (against the door, arms folded), Jack Toothill (fourth left, seated), Edgar Wilkinson (with the ball, captain), Rawson Robertshaw (seated to the right of Wilkinson).

"A TIGHT SCRIMMAGE."

Football is admitted by the majority of people of these days to be a manly and exhilarating pastime for both players and spectators. I go with the majority and endorse the admission. Football is all that, if not more. But I take leave to object to the game when it interferes with business. Those who are familiar with the situation of the *Yorkshireman* office will know that it "hangs out" above the premises of a well-known jewellers' and silversmiths'. One day recently I had important business to transact at the office of this journal. As a matter of fact I had urgent need for interviewing the cashier—and it need hardly be said that I felt desperately annoyed when a surging crowd in front of the silversmiths' in question not only took up the entire pavement but actually made all chance of ingress to the said cashier out of the question. I found the reason for this clustering of the populace in the place indicated was that a number of fine trophies, including the Lancashire League Challenge Cup, were on view in a window. "Confound Fattorini's, and deuce take the Lancashire League!" I said, as, after a vain fight to get through the mob, I reluctantly turned away, minus my interview with the cashier, and, what is worse, minus the "leetle cheque" I was in search of. I'm tired of football now—I'm out of patience with it: the weather is too warm for it; the season has lasted long enough. Out upon football, say I, let it vanish hence and give way to the gentler joys of cricket. It is possible to have too much of a good thing, and when the football season is stretched out so that it reaches all the way from August to May, then I beg leave to suggest that football is putting on overweening airs of importance, and the sooner there is a check put on the thing the better.

Such was the popularity of rugby in Victorian Bradford that even the display of the new Lancashire League Challenge Cup (the Lancashire Club Championship Cup or Senior Competition Cup) in Fattorini's Kirkgate shop window was enough to draw a crowd in 1892.

A rare example of a club rugby programme from 1892. This was one occasion when Bradford fell victims to a southern team, Blackheath. The Blackheath XV was largely made up of internationals.

The rivalry between Bradford and Leeds was strong even in 1892 as this cartoon of a game between the clubs shows. Bradford won this match 24-10 after Leeds had suffered a catastrophic 21-0 defeat by Hunslet the previous week in the Yorkshire Cup final at Fartown.

Thomas Hyde Dobson was the son of Harry Dobson, who trained the 1884 Yorkshire Cup winning side. Tommy was a fine wing and centre who won 5 Yorkshire caps in 1894/95, the last season before the formation of the Northern Union. He was also capped by England against the Scots in 1895. When Bradford went over to the Northern Union in the Great Split of 1895, Tommy was one of the many players who went with them, remaining in the team until 1900.

The most famous painting of rugby is W.B. Wollen's 'Roses Match', which was first exhibited at the Royal Academy in London in the summer of 1895. In November and December 1895 it was exhibited in Bradford and Leeds to great acclaim. Most of the players depicted became Northern Unionists. Three of the most prominent figures were Bradfordians. The player throwing the ball out of the tackle is Manningham's captain Alf Barraclough. Accepting the pass is Bradford forward Jack Toothill and outside him is Tommy Dobson.

Two
Brave New World – The Northern Union 1895-1915

One of the finest forwards to have represented Bradford was John Thomas Toothill, popularly known as Jack. Born at Thornton in 1866, Jack played for Manningham before joining Bradford. He played a dozen times for England as a Rugby Unionist from 1890 to 1894 and won 50 Yorkshire caps between 1888 and 1894. When Bradford turned to the Northern Union, Jack played in their first game against Wakefield Trinity on the wing. Appropriately enough, his last appearance in the red, black and amber was in the Challenge Cup final of 1898 when Bradford lost 0-7 to Batley at Leeds.

COOPER, THE CRACK.

F. W. Cooper is known throughout the country as a crack three-quarter back and a champion sprinter. He has not in his career attained International place, but "hard lines" and not lack of merit are the reasons for his not having won the highest honours. He practically declined a place in the Welsh team in order to try his future with England, and then a difficulty arose which prevented his selection. Cooper is a native of Abergavenny, and resided there until some four years ago. For a while he played with the Abergavenny Steam Press Club, beginning as a half back, and developing into a promising three-quarter back.

F. COOPER.

He also served in certain matches as a full back. Then, playing with Abergavenny until 1892-3, he was noticed by Newport, and passed quickly from the second team in the first rank. He finished his football education in the company of the famous A. J. Gould, and he was similarly talented when he came to Bradford. With Bradford, he had been singularly successful, and was popularly elected captain last season. His football proficiency amounts to a rare gift. He has been a prolific scorer, and heads the list of contributors in the matter of points. At the outset of this season he announced that in view of his splendid prospects as a sprinter, he did not intend to play football again, but he was persuaded to play, and has done as well as ever. Since he won the Booth Hall Plate, Cooper has been regarded by many judges as the coming champion sprinter.—Photo by W. L. Parkinson, of The Grosvenor Studio, Bradford.

Tom Broadley was a Bingley man who carved out a reputation as one of England's greatest forwards. As a Bingley player he won 6 England caps from 1893 to 1896 and 38 for Yorkshire. He also played for the West Riding club, Leeds, before joining Bradford in 1896. A wonderful dribbler of the ball, Broadley could play in any position. In 238 games for Bradford he bagged 48 tries. He retired after playing in Bradford's 5-0 win over Salford at Halifax in the Championship play-off on 28 April 1904. He became a publican at the Punch Bowl, Park Lane, the Fleece Inn, Bingley, and the Manville Arms, Great Horton Road, Bradford.

Fred Cooper was one of the first Welshmen to move to Bradford. Having played for his native Abergavenny and then Newport, he arrived at Park Avenue in 1893. As a wing or centre he was an absolute flyer, so quick, in fact, that he became a national sprint star, winning the coveted Booth Hall Plate. Remarkably, this Welshman played for Yorkshire at both codes of rugby, winning 7 Rugby Union caps and 9 as a Northern Unionist. Fred was a talented goal-kicker, as well as a regular try-scorer, and had the distinction of leading the Northern Union's point-scoring list in its first season with 106 points, sharing the top spot with Manningham's George Lorimer.

Bradford scoured the country for top quality players to maintain their elite status. Amongst several Scots brought south perhaps the most famous was Alex Laidlaw. Laidlaw, a native of Edinburgh, made his name playing for Hawick and appeared for Scotland against Ireland in 1897 before joining Bradford in 1898. He remained a mainstay of the Bradford pack until 1908. In 1906 he converted the only try of the game when Bradford beat Salford 5-0 in the Challenge Cup final at Headingley.

BRADFORD'S CUMBRIAN CRACK.

Bill Eagers was a Cumbrian who signed for Bradford in 1900 from Millom. A brilliantly gifted, if sometimes erratic, full-back or centre, Eagers played for the Park Avenue side for five years. In his first season he earned a winners' medal in the Yorkshire Senior Competition Championship and in 1903/04 helped Bradford to win the First Division Championship. He left Bradford for Hunslet, where he achieved immortality by figuring in their 'all four cups' triumphs in 1907/08.

In 1903/04 Bradford became champions of the Northern Union for the first time. After tying with Salford at the top of the First Division, a play-off for the title was arranged at Thrum Hall, Halifax. Bradford took the title with a 5-0 victory before a crowd of 12,000 – an excellent turnout for a Thursday fixture. From left to right, back row: Robson (trainer), Sinton, Heseltine, Sharratt. Middle row: Hutt, Barker, Greenwood, Smales, Feather, Mosby, Eagers. Front row: Dunbavin, Gunn, Rees, Marsden, Turner, Laidlaw, Dechan. On ground: Surman, Brear.

From 1903 to 1908 Welshman Gomer Gunn was almost a permanent fixture as Bradford's full-back. The strong-tackling former Treherbert player made 178 appearances in five years, scoring a solitary try but landing 41 goals. In 1905 Park Avenue was the venue for the first Northern Union international fixture to be played in Yorkshire, when Gomer kicked a goal in Other Nationalities' 11-26 defeat by England. He is seen wearing his Other Nationalities cap and wearing the jersey he won as a schoolboy for Wales Rugby Union. He later played for Wigan and Keighley.

George Marsden joined Bradford from Morley RUFC in 1900, soon after winning 3 England caps as a fly-half. He developed into one of the finest half-backs of the Edwardian era and was one of the most popular players ever to appear for Bradford. Marsden was skipper of both the triumphant Championship side of 1903/04 and the Challenge Cup winning team of 1906. Defensively he was regarded as practically perfect and a creative player in attack. Having retired in 1906, Marsden reappeared in 1910 for a further three seasons with Northern and even turned out three times in the 1916/17 season.

G. H. MARSDEN.

Bradford beat Salford 5-0 in the 1906 Challenge Cup final at Headingley, after knocking out Wakefield Trinity, Leigh, Halifax and Batley. Interestingly 'a reproduction of the game in animated pictures' was later shown at St George's Hall. From left to right, back row: Hoyle (secretary), Greenwood, Connell, Feather, Smales, Francis, Grayson, Walton, Mosby, Surman, Rees, Farrell (trainer). Middle row: Gunn, Sharratt, Dechan, Marsden, Turner, Laidlaw, Mann. Front row: Dunbavin, Heseltine, Brear.

CARICATURES OF CELEBRITIES.

Mementoes of the 1906 Challenge Cup final. *Above:* Star members of the Salford and Bradford teams in caricature. The Bradford trio are George Marsden, Gomer Gunn and Scottish winger Jimmy Dechan. Six months after the cup final Dechan scored seven tries in a Yorkshire Cup-tie against Bramley at Park Avenue, a club record which is still intact. *Below:* Captains of the two teams, George Marsden (right) and James Lomas, are depicted wrestling for supremacy before an audience of football imps.

CATCH-AS-CATCH-CAN.

Irving (sometimes spelt Erving) Mosby is a largely forgotten figure in Bradford's history but he was a stalwart of the side for a decade from 1901 onward. He was a splendid centre, brilliant in defence, good on attack and a fine goal-kicker. Hailing from Normanton, he made his name with Leicester before landing at Park Avenue. He won 7 Yorkshire caps whilst with Bradford and played for England against Other Nationalities in 1905. He was a member of the Bradford XIII which won the Yorkshire Cup in 1906 after beating Hull KR by 8-5 in the final at Wakefield.

Few men have given better service to Bradford rugby than Tommy Surman, a half-back whose career spanned almost twenty years. He first played at Park Avenue in 1902 and was still a regular in 1921. He saw the good days before the Great Betrayal of 1907, was transferred in 1909 against his wishes to Hull KR, where he remained for five years, and experienced dire days as Northern plumbed the depths. He was a good enough player, however, to win both Yorkshire and England caps.

For two decades from 1884 Bradford were not the only senior club in the district. Their local rivals Manningham may not have had the social standing, financial clout or support of the Park Avenuites, but they were often just as successful on the pitch. Both clubs won the Yorkshire Cup once, both were champions of the Northern Union and Bradford's three successes in the Yorkshire Senior Competition were only one better than Manningham. This is the Manningham team which won the inaugural Northern Union Championship and the YSC in 1895/96. From left to right, back row: Bamford, Jowett, Tolson, Wilkinson, Thomas, Clegg, Procter, Whiteoak, Robson, Wilson. Middle row: Leach, Atkinson, Brown, Barraclough, Lorimer, Padgett, Newton. Front row: Needham, Williamson, Sunderland, Pickles.

The Manningham team of 1899/1900. From left to right, back row: Flockhart, Naylor (secretary), Wilkinson, Jowett, Greenwood, Ayrton, Partington, Wyvill, Barker, Knowles, Leach, Donaldson. Middle row: Bradley, Thomas, Rhodes, Proctor, Whitley, Spivey, Carter. Front row: Taylor, Wade, Gaunt.

Fattorini & Sons, the Bradford jewellers and silversmiths, have had a long association with rugby in Bradford and with the wider game, supplying trophies and medals before and after the Great Split of 1895. This advertisement from around 1905 provides good examples of their wares. The Lancashire Challenge Cup was contested from 1905 to 1992 while the Northern Rugby League medals for 1902/03 were won by Halifax for finishing at the top of Division One. The Yorkshire-New Zealand tasselled medal/badge relates to the All Black Rugby Union fixture played at Leeds.

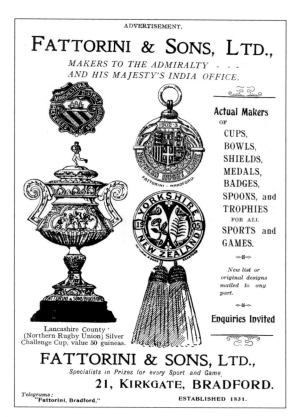

Tony Fattorini was present at the historic meeting at the George Hotel, Huddersfield, in August 1895 when the Northern Union was formed. He was a leading administrator in both the amateur and professional eras, serving Manningham from 1891 until its transformation into Bradford City AFC in 1903. Fattorini served on the committee of the Northern Union from its inception, became president of the Yorkshire Senior Competition in 1899/1900, and president of the Yorkshire County NRU in 1901/02. He was one of the prime movers, however, in enabling soccer to replace rugby at Valley Parade.

A MANN

BRADFORD N.U.

Alf Mann was the last truly outstanding player produced by Bradford before the First World War. A forward of rare vigour and dash with a penchant for scoring crucial tries, Mann became Bradford Northern's first Test player when he figured in the First and Third Tests against Australia in 1908/09. One of his other claims to fame was scoring Bradford's last try under fifteen-a-side rules against Broughton Rangers on 30 April 1906. Along with Tommy Surman he was transferred to Hull KR in 1909, but returned to play for Bradford from 1918 to 1922. This portrait dates from the latter period.

Bradford Northern's fortunes declined rapidly after the Great Betrayal of 1907. Money was in short supply and Northern tempted some great old players who were past their prime to play for them. One of these was Archie Rigg of Halifax, captain of Yorkshire in the early days of the Northern Union and arguably the pre-eminent half-back of his era. Rigg was thirty-six when he came out of retirement in 1908 to play another three seasons for Northern.

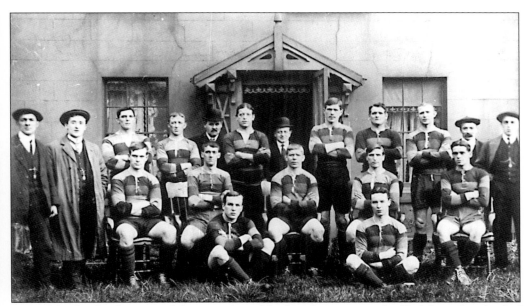

One of the few bright spots of this period was Northern's progess to the Yorkshire Cup final of 1913, their last appearance in any major final for twenty-seven years. The team knocked out Keighley, York and Wakefield Trinity before losing 3-19 to Huddersfield in the final at Halifax on 29 November 1913. This team group shot was taken at Barrow some five weeks prior to the final.

Joe Winterburn, who captained the 1913 Yorkshire Cup final team. He is wearing his Yorkshire cap and jersey, having played in the pack against Cumberland and the Australians in 1908 while a Keighley player. Before joining Keighley he had played for Bradford Victoria Rangers, helping them to lift the Bradford Challenge Cup, the Bradford Charity Cup and the League Shield. His career at Bradford ran from 1911 to 1920.

Jack Bartholomew was another of those players who had seen better days when he came to Birch Lane in 1914. He had been a member of Huddersfield's legendary 'Team of all the Talents' and had toured Australasia with the first Lions in 1910. He gave good service to Bradford, playing mostly at stand-off until 1922. He is wearing his Huddersfield jersey and his tour cap. Jack was the uncle of Eric Morecambe, the comedian.

Three
Dark Days
1919-1938

Don't forget

BRADFORD
NORTHERN
v.
WIGAN

At Birch Lane, Bradford

ON

WED. OCT. 1ST, 1924

Kick Off 4-30 p.m.

A handbill for a game against Wigan – a rare memento of Northern's days at Birch Lane. Wigan finished third in this season while Bradford finished next to bottom of the league. Nevertheless, Bradford earned a surprise 10-10 draw.

LNER

<table>
<tr><td>Rugby League Football Match:</td><td></td><td>BRADFORD v. BRAMLEY.</td></tr>
</table>

Saturday, 8th December, 1923

FOOTBALL EXCURSIONS TO

BRAMLEY

WILL BE RUN AS UNDER:—

FROM	DEPARTURE TIMES.		RETURN FARES— THIRD CLASS.	
	p.m.	p.m.	s.	d.
Bradford (Exchange) -	1 15	2 2	0	8
St. Dunstans - -	1 18	2 5	0	7
Laisterdyke - -	1 24	2 10	0	6
Bramley - arr.	1 30	2 20		

Passengers return on day of issue only from BRAMLEY by any train after 4-0 p.m.

Children under 3 years of age, Free; 3 and under 12, Half-fares. Tickets are not transferable, and will only be available on the date of issue, at the stations named, and by the trains advertised on the bills; if used on any other date, at any other stations, or by any other trains than those named, they will be forfeited and the full ordinary fare will be charged.
NO LUGGAGE ALLOWED.
The Company gives notice that tickets for the s Excursions are issued at a reduced rate, and subject to the condition that the Company shall not be liable for any loss, damage, injury, or delay to passengers arising from any cause whatever.

ENGLISH CUP FINAL—WEMBLEY, 1924.
Parties desiring Saloon accommodation should **MAKE EARLY APPLICATION TO PREVENT DISAPPOINTMENT.**

Tickets can be obtained in advance at the Stations, and at 24, Market Street, Bradford (Tel. No. 490); also from Messrs. DEAN & DAWSON, 83, Market Street, Bradford.

Communications respecting the running of Excursions, and the issue of Week-end or Pleasure Party Tickets, should be addressed to the Company's Town Offices, or to Mr. T. A. PAINTER, District Manager, 66, Wellington Street, Leeds (Telephone No.: Leeds, 20615).

London, King's Cross Station, November, 1923.

25/1,500—19/11/23—P & S., L.—292.   LD 3/24979

For a Programme of Holiday Tours write or call at Dean & Dawson's Offices.

Very few Bradford fans would have taken advantage of this excursion to nearby Bramley. Bramley were the only team to finish below Northern in the 1923/24 season but still beat the Birch Lane men 14-2.

The 1920s saw Bradford still deep in
the financial mire and continuing to
rely on youngsters and old-time stars to
revive fortunes. Jack Beames, the
former Newport RFC, Halifax and Test
back-row forward, was tempted out of
retirement in 1923 aged thirty-three. By
1924 he had retired permanently,
having made only 24 appearances for
the club and scored 4 tries.

Stanley Moorhouse made only five
appearances for Bradford in the 1923/24
season. He never gave any indication of
the form which had made him such a
renowned winger for Huddersfield,
Yorkshire and England in a glorious career
between 1909 and 1922, when his
partnership with the sublime Harold
Wagstaff had been one of the wonders of
the Northern Union.

Slightly more productive for Bradford was Moorhouse's fellow Fartown winger, Albert Rosenfeld, the greatest try-scorer the Northern Union had produced, whose 80 tries in the 1913/14 season has never been matched. Rozzy played 23 games for Northern in seasons 1923/24 and 1924/25 but scored a solitary try in a 12-8 home victory over Wigan Highfield on 26 January 1924.

Bradford Northern had a comparatively successful season in 1925/26 but still only finished twenty-third of the twenty-seven teams in the league. They met Batley at Mount Pleasant on 9 September 1925 and lost 6-23. One of their tries was this effort from stand-off Teddy Melling. The other Bradford players are Hughes, Gomersall, Dobson and Webster, who scored the side's other try.

Four days earlier on 5 September 1925 Bradford had better luck when they defeated Leigh 7-0 at Birch Lane. Winger Gledhill is passing the ball to scrum-half Hughes (7). Agar, Dobson, Smith and Brett are the other Bradford players. The crowd for this match, the first of the season, was reported to be around 5,000, which was about double the average for Bradford in this period. By the season's close, Bradford were £1,580 in debt, a massive amount, particularly as these were days of economic depression. The club was constantly being bailed out by loans from the Rugby Football League, making public appeals for funds and trying all manner of money-raising schemes. Ultimately, though, they always had to sell their most promising players. The 1925/26 season did, however, throw up one terrific windfall for the club's finances when a local derby against Keighley in the first round of the Challenge Cup was scheduled for 13 February 1926. The clubs agreed to play at Valley Parade and, although Keighley were to finish next to bottom of the league, a crowd of 20,973 gathered to watch two basement clubs fight out a 2-2 draw. The replay, another draw (5-5), was also played at Valley Parade. Northern eventually progressed to the second round by winning the second replay 9-4 at Leeds.

The Bradford team early in the 1925/26 season. From left to right: Mereweather (trainer), Kirkham, Brett, Hughes, Gledhill, Agar, Melling, Gomersall, Shaw (director), Mills, Webster, Davy (director), Dobson, Moran, Redmond, Smith, Waddilove (chairman), Clifford (assistant trainer). While the crowds to watch these players at Birch Lane rarely exceeded a few thousand in 1925/26, they were more than enough to cause serious disorder problems on a couple of occasions. Two weeks after a particularly troublesome game against Dewsbury on 17 April 1926, the Rugby Football League Management Committee ordered Bradford to close the Birch Lane ground for the first two games of the 1926/27 season. They were instructed to play these games at least five miles away from Bradford. Consequently, their home game against Halifax was played at Halifax (lost 10-48) and the game against York was taken to Keighley (lost 7-13).

Teddy Melling, depicted here on a cigarette card in Ogden's 'Famous Rugby Players' set, was one of the few genuinely gifted players in Northern's ranks in the dark days of the 1920s. A Wiganer, he joined Bradford from Batley in 1920 and played 286 games for the club in eight years, scoring 339 points. The £300 Bradford received for his transfer to Broughton Rangers in 1928 was definitely a lucrative return on their investment.

Even Teddy Melling, seated centre, could not lead this 1926/27 team to a position higher than next to bottom, below Pontypridd and above only Castleford. Only 6 of 36 league games were won and no team defended as badly as Bradford, who let in 652 points.

After exchanging work down a Cumbrian pit for a job in a Bradford mill in 1926, loose forward Harold Young created his own niche in history by becoming Bradford Northern's first Australasian tourist in 1928. A skilled Cumberland wrestler, he excelled in tackling. Soon after returning from the tour Bradford sold him to Huddersfield to alleviate yet another financial crisis. He did, however, eventually return to Bradford in December 1933 and retired in 1935, by which time the club had settled at Odsal and were looking at a brighter future.

Harold Young remained a resident of Bradford until his death in 1996. Aged ninety-six, at the time he was the oldest surviving British Lion. He is pictured here in 1995 with a portrait of himself wearing an England jersey and a Cumberland cap, the county for which he made 16 appearances.

Arguably the most talented native-born Bradford Rugby League player was Stanley Brogden, who excelled as a centre, winger and stand-off. Although weighing just over ten stones, his speed and elusiveness constantly nonplussed opponents. He was a month past his seventeenth birthday when he first played for Northern in 1927, but 62 appearances and barely two and a half years later, he was sold to Huddersfield for a massive fee of £1,000. Northern again had to sell in order to survive. Stanley did return to play 33 games as a guest for Northern during the Second World War.

S. BROGDEN, the brilliant English footballer. Watch him tomorrow.

HARRY CAMPBELL

Stanley Brogden in caricature as a British Lion. Brogden won 16 Test caps, 15 England caps and 19 Yorkshire caps. He was a British Lion in 1932 and 1936, and many critics believed he played his best rugby on the hard grounds of Australia, which suited his phenomenal pace.

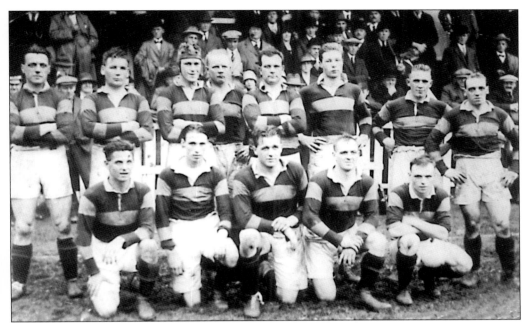

Northern rose from twenty-eighth to sixteenth in the 1927/28 league table before finishing bottom for four consecutive seasons. If this team could have been retained for longer, prospects would have been brighter. The four shining lights in this team had all been sold within a couple of years: Harold Young (back row, fourth left), Jack Cox (back row, sixth left), Teddy Melling (back row, extreme right) and the boyish Stanley Brogden (front row, second left).

The 1932/33 team must have been one of the first English Rugby League teams to wear chevrons on their shirts, a style which later became almost synonymous with the game. For the first time in five years the club got off the bottom of the league, finishing five places higher. From left to right, back row: Thornburrow, Parr, Elson, Litt, McLester, Taylor, Sutton. Front row: Townsend, Walker, Bradbury, Smith, Sherwood, Bush.

By CENTRE

Bradford Northern ....7pts.   Australians .... 5pts.

A DROPPED goal by Sherwood with the last kick of the match gave Bradford Northern a most unexpected victory over the Australians at Valley Parade, by two goals and a try (7 points) to a goal and a try (5 points).

It was a sensational climax but it merely produced a deserving reward to a team that played desperately hard to achieve the honour of being the first club side to overcome the tourists. Two wet days—two defeats after 11 successive victories under dry conditions—has an obvious inference. The Australians, playing only five members of their first team, were what I can best describe as "lost."

Sherwood

They struggled in a vain effort to overcome conditions which are more or less foreign to them, and failed.

ALWAYS DEFENDING

Throughout the second half in pouring rain on a ground offering an insecure foothold and with a ball well-nigh impossible to handle, the Australians, hopelessly beaten in the scrums and menaced by inspired opponents at every turn, scarcely moved from defence.

The Northern forwards played the game of their lives. One or two of them had almost spent themselves, but they carried on ultimately to win their reward.

It was, however, a match which only a case-hardened Rugby man could enjoy. It lacked all the finer touches of the game. Bradford knowing their own weaknesses, would have made it a forward game in any circumstances and it requires little imagination to realise that under the prevailing conditions their six scrummagers became a dominating power.

NO ADAPTABILITY

The Australians revealed no adaptability. The pack they played in this game would have met with trouble even on a dry ground because they were pushed off the ball five times out of six.

It was Glasheen's first match and he was beaten by a crafty opponent in Turner, who did not hesitate to squat, swing and do all the things a hooker should not do.

To make matters worse for the tourists Dempsey, playing in the second row, sustained a severe injury to his ribs mid-way in the second half and should have retired, and why the Australians should stand in the rain for more than five minutes at the interval while the Bradford players retired to their rooms for a refresher. I do not know.

The fact nevertheless remains that Bradford always appeared the more likely team in the second half to win. Their style, of course, was vigorous, and perhaps crude, in comparison with the ill-conceived notion of the Tourists that they could win by open football; but it was sound tactically and produced the desired result.

Sherwood, the loose forward, who dropped the goal, played superbly from start to finish, tackling with magnificent determination and inspiring his colleagues. The giant Litt, Turner and Sutton in the front row, with Parr and Elson in support, played heroically.

Not for 30 years, since the days when the old Manningham club played at Valley Parade, has there been such a triumphant Rugby demonstration as when Sherwood won this game.

ALL-ROUND POWER

I was more than surprised, too, by the general power of the Bradford team. What they did in this game they should be able to repeat.

The supporting tactics—obviously taught by the inimitable Ben Gronow—were excellent. Bush and Bradbury were two clever half-backs, and what the three-quarter line lacked in modern attacking science they made up for in defence.

Walker and Halton did especially well, and Taylor, without being brilliant, was a sound full-back.

DISAPPOINTING DISPLAY

The Australian team which earlier in the day had been given a civic reception by the Lord Mayor (Alderman J. W. Longley) gave a disappointing display.

No doubt the principal cause of the decline was the weather which kept the attendance down to 3,000, but another reason—and for which they can be forgiven for the Northern certainly played above themselves—was that they underestimated the power of their opponents.

They should not have hesitated to alter their original formation of their pack when they saw the state of the ground and the weather. It was a fatal error to have brought Glasheen out as hooker for the first time on such a day.

Every attack they made, with the exception of the one which brought their try, was driven out over the touch-line and dribbling they must practice if they are going to hold their own on the mud patches which will be fashionable for the remainder of their tour.

EARLY LEAD

Litt, with a penalty goal, gave Bradford the lead five minutes after the start. Four minutes later Neumann, their flying centre—he went on the wing in the second half—cut through the centre and served Prigg, who deceived no less than four opponents into the belief that he was aiming for the corner. Instead he stopped dead in his stride and simply walked over. Mead adding the goal points.

The lead was in the possession of the Tourists exactly 11 minutes before Bradbury equalised, gathering the ball from a five-yards scrum and simply hurling himself over the line for an equalising try which Litt failed to improve.

At the interval the scores were level and remained so until Sherwood's last-minute dropped goal. Litt missed two penalty shots and at a rough estimate Bradford attacked for 30 minutes out of the 40. Bush, Sherwood and Halton were injured in the struggle, but none so seriously as Dempsey, who was ill-advised in continuing to play.

Bradford N.—Taylor; Tetlow, Berry, Halton, Walker; Bush, Bradbury; Litt, Turner, Sutton, Parr, Elson, Sherwood.

Australia.—Smith; Pearce (C.), Laws, Neumann, Gardner; Doonar, Mead, Curran, Glasheen, Dempsey, O'Connor, Doyle, Prigg.

Referee: Mr J. W. Webb (Broughton).

ALMOST A DOUBLE

Australian Tourists Score Winning Try in Last Three Minutes

By CENTRE

Bradford Northern .... 7pts.   Australia .... 10pts.

BRADFORD NORTHERN in their second match against the Australians at Valley Parade went very near to completing the "double." Until 22 minutes off the end of another hard and thrilling match they led by five points.

Then the Australians equalised and, unlike the first encounter, when Sherwood gave the Northern a sensational win with the last kick of the match, on this occasion it was Doyle who attained the winning points for the tourists three minutes from the end.

COPIED BRADFORD'S IDEA

Had the Australians adhered to their normal tactics they would assuredly have failed, for the tackling and spotting of the Bradford players was of such an enthusiastic character that no attack could possibly have matured by close-passing methods.

In the last 20 minutes they copied the Bradford idea to a certain extent of following up long kicks and using their speed. **Brown, who kicked a couple of goals, had the satisfaction of breaking the score record of previous Tourists held by Weissell (1929) and Horder (1921), who both obtained 127 points.**

TOURISTS' DEFENCE 'AT SEA"

When Bradbury gave Bradford the lead with a try scored at the corner, the Australian defence after 11 minutes' 'hammering" was all at sea."

Going round on the blind side from a five-yards scrum, the Bradford captain was unopposed. It was a remarkably simple affair, but deserving of the highest praise for its subtlety.

When Litt kicked a goal from the touchline enthusiasm knew no bounds.

The success acted as a wonderful incentive and until Brown placed his first goal—a penalty—after 20 minutes the close-order play and wonderful tackling of the home players more or less confined the " Kangaroos " to their own quarter.

MISSED CHANCE

In one raid however, I thought that Stehr missed a chance—the only one the Australians had during the first half—of scoring a try, when he mulled the ball from a pass by Curran.

Towards the interval the Australians rallied—though such was the enthusiasm of the Northern forwards that they pushed their opponents back fully 10 yards in loose scrummage formation.

LITT'S WONDERFUL GOAL

It was no more than the home players deserved when Litt with a wonderful kick from near half-way gave his side the lead following an off-side offence by Thicknesse.

Leading 7-2 at the interval Bradford played for the first 15 minutes against the wind with such confidence and determination that they not only seemed certain to hold the advantage but likely to increase it.

Prigg made a remarkable save from a mass of Northern forwards on his own line. **Then came the change of ideas by the Tourists and after Brown had hit one of the posts with a penalty shot, Prigg dived through a scrum near the line for a try which Brown improved to equalise.**

The remaining 22 minutes were fought with amazing determination.

The more I praise the Australians for a fine exhibition, the more credit is due to the Northern team of artisan footballers who ran them so closely.

ALL PLAYED WELL

Every man played his part, with Bradbury outstanding in the Northern side and Prigg pre-eminent for the Tourists.

For stern, relentless endeavour by both sides it was a match to remember.

Bradford Northern.—Taylor; Tetlow, Halton, Berry, Walker; Thornburrow, Bradbury; Litt, Turner, Sutton, Parr, Elson, Sherwood.

Australians.—McMillan; Ridley, Why, Brown, Neumann; Hey, Thicknesse; Curran, Folwell, Stehr, O'Connor, Doyle, Prigg.

Referee: Mr. A. E. Harding (Manchester).

There were 10,000 spectators, the receipts being £797.

Opposite and above: On 11 October 1933 Bradford Northern caused the sensation of the season by beating the touring Australians 7-5 at Valley Parade. Northern were in their customary position at the foot of the league table while the Kangaroos had won their eleven opening fixtures before losing the First Test four days prior to meeting Bradford. The Australians were so taken aback that they asked for a rematch, which again took place at Valley Parade on 30 October. Again Northern performed undreamed of heroics but finally suffered a narrow defeat by a near Test strength thirteen. These match reports make fascinating reading.

Bradford Northern in 1934/35. From left to right, back row: Smith (chairman), Green, Morgan, Webb, Winnard, Pilling, Sherwood, Hutchinson, Gronow (trainer). Front row: Dobson (director), Bush, Carmichael, Hayes, Young, Goulthorpe, Wilson, Dilorenzo, Ingleby (director), -?-.

In 1935/36 Bradford Northern finished in nineteenth position in the league, their best performance since 1927/28. Although apparently a mediocre performance, it marked the start of a long overdue return to better days. The team, pictured on an Ardath cigarette photo-card, is, from left to right, back row: Higson, Winnard, Morgan, Chadwick, Carmichael, Moore, Orford, Jones. Front row: Billington, Spillane, Jackson, Grainge, Hutchinson.

Tom Winnard was signed from St Helens in 1933 for a club record fee of £385. It was money well spent as this outstanding centre was one of the rocks on which a new, aspiring team was built. He became the first Bradford Northern player to score 1,000 points in a career which stretched until 1944. In 1936/37 he set a club record by amassing 240 points, which consisted of 22 tries and 87 goals. This portrait comes from a cigarette card in Ogden's 'Football Club Captains' series.

OGDEN'S CIGARETTES

T. WINNARD (BRADFORD NORTHERN)

Winnard had been capped by Lancashire in 1933 as a St Helens player and, unusually for those days, won another two caps while a Bradford player. The pinnacle of his career, however, came when he played for England against France at Halifax in 1937, ironically a game which was transferred from Odsal because of waterlogging. He is seen here running at full pelt, surrounded by three Frenchmen.

Len Higson was a tower of strength in the Bradford front row between 1935 and 1947. He had won Yorkshire honours with Leeds and Wakefield Trinity prior to joining Northern. He was finally capped by England against Wales at Odsal in 1941 when the BBC broadcast the second half to a war-weary populace. He played in all Bradford's big matches during the war, helping the club to win all the available honours. On retiring he joined the coaching staff at Odsal.

A prime example of the better type of player being attracted to Odsal in the mid-1930s was Ted Spillane. Spillane, a native of Dunedin in New Zealand, had made his name with Wigan and Keighley. He was adept at wing, centre and stand-off and was a good captain. Between 1934 and 1937 he made 101 appearances for Bradford but more importantly set the right standards in a team which was beginning to blossom.

Ernest Pollard arrived at Odsal in September 1937, via Wakefield Trinity and Leeds, holding the record for most points in a season for both clubs. A stand-off or centre of the highest class, he had toured Australasia in 1932 and had been capped by Yorkshire when only nineteen. Ernest struck up a wonderfully productive centre partnership with Tom Winnard in 1937/38, scoring 95 points himself while Winnard bagged 152. His career ended tragically in October 1938, however, when he suffered a severe knee injury aged twenty-eight. In later life he became a primary school head teacher.

Des Case, a teenage winger from Wales, joined Northern in the same month that Pollard did. Case was one of a legion of Welsh players who trekked to Bradford in the 1930s and 1940s and he was one of the most successful. He enjoyed eleven years with Bradford during which he played 193 games, scoring 79 tries and 10 goals despite the interruptions of the war, which saw him posted to India with the Royal Signals. His last official games for Bradford were the Challenge Cup and Championship finals of 1948, after which he returned to Wales as an insurance agent for the Co-op.

The 1938/39 Northern team represented a bridge between the dark old days and the revitalisation of the club in the 1940s. From left to right, back row: Winnard, Smith, Dilorenzo,

Pollard, Case, Moore, Orford, Higson. Front row: Bennett, Carmichael, Hayes, Grainge, Harrison.

G. CARMICHAEL (BRADFORD N.)

Although Northern were established at Odsal, the club had to use Valley Parade twice within a few days in 1937. Odsal was so saturated that the second round Challenge Cup-tie with Huddersfield was postponed on 27 February. Conditions remained so dire that on 3 March the game had to be played at Valley Parade, ending in a 12-2 defeat before a crowd of 19,387. This shot of Northern charging down a Huddersfield kick indicates that ground conditions were not much better at Valley Parade! Three days later Bradford beat Oldham 27-10 in a league match on the same ground, by which time the crowd had fallen to 5,116.

George Carmichael certainly made his mark at Odsal. He joined Bradford from Hull KR in 1934 and went on to make 481 appearances for the Odsalites before retirement in 1950. A steady, reliable full-back, George was also keen to link up with the attack and he won his fair share of games for Northern with a tally of over 400 goals.

Four

Odsal Stadium –
Field of Dreams or
Impossible Dream?

On 1 April 1939 Odsal held its first record crowd for an English Rugby League match of 64,453 when Halifax met Leeds in a Challenge Cup semi-final. This was the view toward the new stand as Leeds defended the Rooley Avenue end.

An empty Odsal in 1936, showing the reverse view of the ground from overleaf. This shot gives an indication of the distance players had to walk before and after games en route to and from the dressing rooms. These were situated in the buildings at the top left of the picture and the players sometimes had to make their way through massive and emotional crowds – no wonder police escorts were sometimes needed! The fragile fencing was replaced with much sturdier wooden palisades by 1939.

An aerial view of Odsal in August 1934, shortly before Bradford met Huddersfield in the ground's first game on 1 September. Northern lost that fixture 16-31 before a crowd estimated at 20,000.

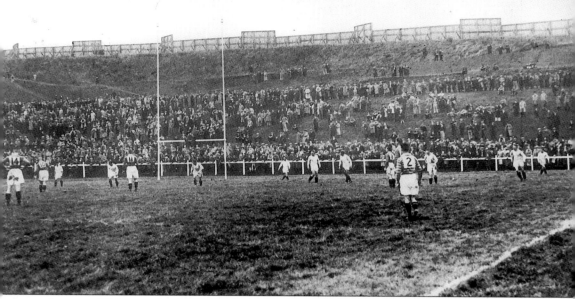

A year later, on 28 September 1935, Bradford defeated Huddersfield 9-3 before another sizable crowd, which nonetheless seems fairly sparse in the vastness of the Rooley Avenue embankments. Bradford (in white shirts) are just about to take a 25-yard drop-out.

Odsal staged its first major final on 22 October 1938 when Huddersfield beat Hull 18-10 in the Yorkshire Cup final. A crowd of 28,714, the biggest for a Yorkshire Cup final since 1922, was present. The Huddersfield and Hull teams are lined out prior to kick-off. The famous Wigan referee, Frank Fairhurst, holds the ball.

In 1944 Odsal hosted a very special occasion when a Combined Services Rugby League team met a Combined Services Rugby Union team under fifteen-a-side laws. The programme cover for this game was a version of a design which was used for many big wartime games at Odsal. The Rugby League XV won the game 15-10. War charities benefited to the tune of around £1,500 from a crowd estimated at 13,000-15,000.

Willie Davies, the Bradford Northern stand-off, was originally selected to captain the Combined Services Rugby League XV but had to pull out. Bradford-born Stanley Brogden (Hull) replaced Davies and scored the match-winning try. Northern's Trevor Foster took over the captaincy and there was also a place for Ernest Ward at full-back. Interestingly, on the Union XV left wing was E.S. Simpson, a member of Bradford RUFC. Willie Davies, one of the greatest of all stand-offs, regularly played for RAF and Combined Services sides during the war and captained Wales on occasions.

Wartime regulations and the fear of air raids caused Odsal's capacity to be reduced drastically in the Second World War. Even so, the ground continued to house the largest crowds allowed. This action from a cup-tie against Halifax in 1942 shows a sizeable audience in the background. The capacity for the 1941 Challenge Cup final, featuring Halifax versus Leeds, was set at and reached 28,500 and was officially the largest crowd during the war, although Bradford Northern's second leg Challenge Cup final against Wigan in 1944 was reported to have drawn 30,000.

The New Zealand and Great Britain teams, led by Pat Smith and Joe Egan, make the long trek from the dressing rooms to the pitch before the third and deciding Test of the 1947 series. This was the first Test to be staged at Odsal, a decision totally justified by the record British Test crowd of 42,685, who saw a 25-9 victory for the home team.

On 29 January 1949 Great Britain defeated Australia 23-9 in the final Test of the series. It was Odsal's first Ashes Test and the crowd of 42,000 was a record for a home Ashes Test. Bradford's Ernest Ward captained the British XIII and scored eleven of their points. In this shot of the Low Moor End the British players move away from their line after an Australian conversion has failed.

A new ground record was established at the 1950 Challenge Cup semi-final. An attendance of 69,898 descended on Odsal's bowl and saw Warrington defeat Leeds 16-4. Leeds centre Bob Bartlett is about to be tackled by Warrington centre Ally Naughton. Ike Proctor and Dickie Wiliams of Leeds and Warrington's Gerry Helme are the other players in view.

Odsal became something of a hoodoo venue for Leeds in this period. The Challenge Cup semi-final of 1951 proved no luckier for them than those of 1939 and 1950, although they did at least manage a 14-14 draw with Barrow before a crowd of 57,459. Barrow won the replay at Fartown 28-13. Two of the game's all-time great stand-off halves, Dickie Williams and Willie Horne, lead their men through Odsal's masses.

On 14 March 1953 the largest crowd ever to watch Bradford Northern at Odsal turned out for the third round Challenge Cup-tie against Huddersfield. The initial figure for the crowd was given as 71,164 but this was later reduced to 69,429. This figure remains a record for a club fixture, excluding semi-finals and final ties. The rival captains, Russ Pepperell and Trevor Foster, seem too busy talking to notice the throng. Northern lost 7-17.

Odsal provided the 1951 Kiwis with the two biggest crowds of their tour. The first Test pulled in a crowd of 37,475 to see Britain win 21-15 while the game against Bradford Northern, billed by the programme as 'The North's First Floodlit Match', attracted 29,072 for what was then regarded as a novelty. Northern recorded a famous 13-8 victory.

Bradford's pioneering involvement with floodlit Rugby League attracted a great deal of media attention but other clubs – Leigh excepted – were always resistant to playing under lights as they argued that Bradford would have an unfair advantage. By today's standards the lights were dull but cost-effective when they were switched on for attractive representative fixtures. Philips Electrical Ltd of Leeds installed the lights within five days of the decision to have them. This atmospheric image shows that even a Bradford training night could attract spectators.

By 1960 the Odsal floodlights were past redemption, ruined by a combination of the weather and Northern's creeping penury. The last games played under them were the final game of the 1960 World Cup – Great Britain versus The Rest of the World on 10 October – and a Yorkshire Cup semi-final between Keighley and Wakefield Trinity two days later. It was not until 29 November 1979 that floodlit Rugby League returned to Odsal when St Helens were the visitors in a league game won 13-9 by Northern, who went on to win the First Division Championship. The new lights, this time on pylons at each corner of the ground, cost £40,000.

Test Rugby League continued to be played at Odsal throughout the 1950s with New Zealand always popular visitors. Here, the Kiwis walk out for the Second Test of 1955 with former Bradford Northern star Bob Hawes second from the right in the Kiwi line. The attendance of 24,443 was the biggest of the twenty-six-match tour of England.

Rugby League — First Division

First Floodlit Match

BRADFORD NORTHERN

VERSUS

ST. HELENS

Match Sponsors to-night
Rawson Bacon Supplies
Phone Bradford 390919

TUESDAY
27th November, 1979
Kick-off 7.30 p.m.

To-night's
MITRE MATCHBALL
Sponsored by
Greenbank Construction Co Building Contractors
Phone Bradford 34415

Souvenir Programme 20p

THE RUGBY LEAGUE
CHALLENGE CUP COMPETITION
FINAL TIE
HALIFAX v. WARRINGTON

(Photo by courtesy of the Yorkshire Post)

ODSAL STADIUM, BRADFORD
WEDNESDAY, 5th MAY, 1954

Official Programme   -   Sixpence

Undoubtedly, the 1954 Challenge Cup final replay between Halifax and Warrington was Odsal's most momentous occasion. The official paying attendance for this game was 102,569 but many thousands more gained free admission by going through broken gates and over wooden fencing. A more likely estimate of the crowd was 120,000 and some authorities would say that this is still an underestimation. Even more amazing is the fact that the game was played on a Wednesday evening after the first game at Wembley had been a try-less boring draw. This programme cover for the replay shows Warrington's Brian Bevan facing the challenge of Halifax's Stan Kielty at Wembley.

The view from the Rooley Avenue End on this remarkable still, taken from a newsreel film, gives some indication of the enormous crowd which assembled for a game which now exists in the game's folklore simply as 'the Odsal replay'. The old chap in the foreground may well have been wondering why he did not arrive earlier.

The view from ground level at the Low Moor End also gives graphic evidence of the multitudes. Warrington are behind their own posts as Halifax's full-back Tuss Griffiths lands a penalty.

The Odsal replay was a much better game than the Wembley match. Warrington won 8-4, with the match-winning try being scored by scrum-half Gerry Helme, seen here grinning broadly after touching down. Note the crowd, several deep, sitting and standing right up to the edge of the playing area. Despite the vastness of the crowd and the primitiveness of the ground, at least by modern standards, no untoward incidents were recorded.

From 1957 to 1962 Odsal housed six Championship finals which drew a combined audience of 345,366. Over 62,000 attended the first of these finals in 1957 when Oldham won a dramatic game against Hull 15-14. Oldham's centre Dennis Ayres goes over for a try supported by Sid Little and watched by Matt Coates, the referee.

In 1958 it was Hull's turn to lift the Championship before a crowd of 57,699. They vanquished a valiant Workington Town by 20-3. Town were leading 3-0 when their second rower Cec Thompson was stretchered off after twenty-five minutes and the remaining twelve men could not hold a powerful Hull side. Hull full-back Peter Bateson is seen converting one of his team's four tries. Workington forwards Stamper, Eve and Edgar are under the crossbar.

One of Rugby League's classic games was the 1959 Championship final when St Helens beat Hunslet 44-22. The Hunslet winger Willie Walker, who joined the reformed Bradford Northern in 1964, is seen racing in the shadow of the old stand pursued by Tom Vollenhoven, whose hat-trick of tries included one of the greatest ever seen at Odsal.

The 1960 Championship final demonstrated Odsal's capacity for housing massive crowds yet again as 83,190, the largest ever outside the Challenge Cup, thronged the stadium. Wigan crushed Wakefield Trinity 27-3 after Neil Fox was injured early on and spent the game limping on the wing. Here, the captains, Derek Turner and Eric Ashton, lead out their teams.

Another 50,000-plus crowd attended the 1961 Championship final when Leeds beat Warrington 25-10. Remarkably, Leeds had never won the Rugby League Championship until that afternoon when Lewis Jones inspired his team to a comfortable win. Leeds centre Derek Hallas is pictured crashing over for one of his two tries. Referee Ron Gelder is in no doubt as to its validity.

An awful afternoon and the apparent certainty of a Wakefield Trinity victory conspired to keep the attendance for the 1962 final down to 37,451. Underdogs Huddersfield, however, had not read the script and ran out 14-5 winners to prevent Trinity from taking all four cups. Huddersfield skipper Tommy Smales (pictured) scored a try and had one of the games of his life. Smales later became a firm favourite at Odsal when he captained Bradford to success in the 1965 Yorkshire Cup final.

In 1960 the World Cup was staged in England for the first time and Odsal was the scene of three of the games. On 24 September Britain beat New Zealand 23-8 in front of 20,577. Oldham centre Alan Davies is pictured crossing for a try at the Rooley Avenue End. Also in evidence are Odsal's trackside seats, the steps leading to the pitch and a BBC outside broadcast van.

Two weeks later, on a foul Saturday afternoon, Great Britain met Australia in what was effectively the World Cup final. The crowd at Odsal was 32,773, the highest of the tournament. It was a brutal match which ended in a 10-3 victory for Great Britain. Here, scrum-half Alex Murphy and an Australian flounder in the mire as the ball goes loose. Billy Boston, one of Britain's try-scorers, races to recover the ball.

67

The 1961 series against New Zealand provided a huge shock when the Kiwis won the First Test at Leeds 29-11. Only 19,980 turned up for the Second Test at Odsal to see Britain turn the tables with a 23-10 triumph. Great Britain second rower, Johnny Whiteley, is captured in spectacular action, tackling Kiwi captain Don Hammond. Bob Dagnall and Abe Terry are the other Britons in close attendance.

For the first time both Challenge Cup semi-finals were played on the same ground in 1962. Wakefield Trinity beat Featherstone Rovers 9-0 before 43,625 on Wednesday 11 April, while 31,423 were at Odsal three days later to see Huddersfield pip Hull KR 6-0. Wakefield's prop Jack Wilkinson is robbed of a try by Rovers' full-back Jack Fennell (with the ball) and prop Malcolm Dixon. Milan Kosanovic, Trinity's Yugoslavian hooker and a former Bradford player, and Don Fox (on ground) await developments.

In 1969 the Championship final was returned to Odsal after a seven-year absence. The attendance of 28,442 was well short of the halcyon years but the clash between Castleford and Leeds had everything: wonderful attacking play, murderous defensive tactics, fluctuating scorelines, a sending-off and this match-winning try by Leeds left winger John Atkinson with only five minutes remaining. Cas right winger Trevor Briggs chases in vain as Atkinson's converted try gives Leeds a 16-14 victory.

The only game that Odsal staged in the 1970 World Cup was France versus Australia. Australia were supposed to walk it and only just over 6,000 fans turned up. They witnessed the shock of the tournament and one of the most entertaining international matches ever staged as France won 17-15. The French tackling was superb as Australian centre superstar Bobby Fulton clearly found to his cost.

By the late 1970s Odsal was no longer one of the game's preferred big match venues. In 1978 it staged its last Challenge Cup semi-final, when Leeds beat Featherstone Rovers 14-9 before only 12,824. Leeds centre Neil Hague is seen scoring a crucial try under the posts having avoided John Newlove's tackle. Referee Stan Wall confirms the touchdown.

New Zealander Tony Coll runs at the British defence in the Second Test of the 1980 series. The Kiwis won 12-8 in the last Test match to be staged at Odsal. Although the crowd was a miserly 10,946, it was the biggest of the series. The last Ashes Test to be played at Odsal was in 1978 and the last Test against France in 1972. The Bradford Northern second rower Jeff Grayshon is the man about to tackle Coll. Others in sight are Glyn Shaw, Fred Lindop (referee), Len Casey and Harry Pinner.

Five
Days of Glory
1939-1953

The Bradford side which beat Warrington 11-7 in the 1947 Challenge Cup semi-final at Swinton. From left to right, back row: Tyler, Evans, Whitcombe, Batten, Smith, Foster. Middle row: Kitching, Darlison, E. Ward, Walters, Carmichael. Front row: Davies, D. Ward. The same thirteen played in the final at Wembley against Leeds.

MR. HARRY HORNBY

ERNEST WARD

GEORGE CARMICHAEL

BARRY TYLER

DAI REES, TEAM MANAGER

A.W. WOOD TRAINER

FRANK WHITCOMBE

BRADFORD NORTHERN R.L. FOOTBALL CLUB

Caricatures of Odsal personalities of the 1946/47 season. The artist, 'Thack', produced them for *The Yorkshire Evening Post*.

Northern's twin godheads of the 1940s: Trevor Foster and Ernest Ward. The two toured Australasia together with the 1946 Lions and are seen wearing their tour caps. With Foster leading the pack and Ward captaining the side from centre, Northern enjoyed a golden age under these two all-time greats.

A nasty landing for a Warrington player in the Championship final of 1948 at Maine Road, Manchester. Throwing him over his shoulder is Bradford prop Frank Whitcombe. Whitcombe played for Northern from 1938 to 1949, later becoming a director at Odsal. A massive man, who helped his hooker to gain vital possession at the scrummages, Frank represented Wales on 14 occasions and was a British Lion in 1946. He played in three successive Wembley finals in 1947, 1948 and 1949, winning the Lance Todd Trophy in 1948.

The 1948/49 Challenge Cup and Yorkshire Cup winners. From left to right, back row: Tyler, Radford, Greaves, Traill, Foster, Jenkins. Front row: Walters, Davies, D. Ward, E. Ward, Leake, Edwards, Whitcombe.

Wembley 1947 marked the start of a remarkable run of three consecutive Challenge Cup finals for Bradford Northern. They were the first team to perform such a feat in the Wembley era. Ernest Ward received the Challenge Cup from the Duke of Gloucester in the Royal Box after Leeds were defeated 8-4.

Bearing away the spoils. Leeds have been vanquished and the Challenge Cup heads for the Bradford dressing room, held aloft by Ernest Ward. Alongside him are full-back George Carmichael, winger Eric Batten and team manager Dai Rees. Sixteen years earlier at the same venue, Rees had carried off the Challenge Cup as captain of Halifax after their victory over York.

Eric Batten scored 165 tries for Bradford Northern between 1943 and 1951. In total he scored 443 tries in a career which stretched from 1933 to 1954 and took him to Wakefield Trinity, Hunslet, Leeds and Featherstone Rovers, as well as Odsal. Few of those tries would have been of more importance than this touchdown at Headingley. It helped Northern to overcome Hunslet 14-7 in the Challenge Cup semi-final of 3 April 1948. A crowd of 38,125 watches the Hunslet winger Ted Carroll arrive too late to stop Eric.

Three weeks later Bradford went to Wigan in the Championship semi-final for a rehearsal of the 1948 Challenge Cup final. They pulled off a stunning 15-3 victory before a Central Park crowd of 32,800. This time Eric Batten is seen in defensive mode, preparing to block a kick from Cec Mountford while Ernest Ward looks on and Des Case lurches toward Mountford. If Bradford fans thought the result was a good omen for the encounter with Wigan at Wembley a week later on 1 May 1948, they were sorely mistaken.

The 1948 Challenge Cup final was the first Rugby League match to be attended by a reigning monarch. It was also witnessed by a world record crowd of 91,465 who paid another world record for receipts of £21,121. In the event, Bradford and Wigan found the occasion too big and a poor game ensued from which Wigan emerged 8-3 winners. King George VI is seen shaking hands with left winger Alan Edwards, who scored Bradford's only try. The other players are Ernest Ward (obscured by the King), Batten, Case, Davies, Donald Ward, Whitcombe and Darlison.

The programme for the 1948 Challenge Cup final was an excellent souvenir of a historic event. However, there was a certain amount of dissatisfaction as the price had doubled from the previous year from six pence to a shilling.

The Bradford and Wigan teams stride out at Wembley for the 1948 Challenge Cup final. The Northern team is, from left to right: Traill, Tyler, Foster, Smith, Darlison, Whitcombe, D. Ward, Davies, Edwards, Case, Batten, Leake, E. Ward.

Bradford found it difficult to shake off the stubborn Wigan defence in a game which was marred by drizzle and a treacherous surface. On this occasion Bradford hooker Vic Darlison (9) struggles to break free from Wigan winger Gordon Ratcliffe. Ironically, Darlison had been a Wigan player before joining Bradford in the 1942/43 season.

Bradford's third successive Wembley final in 1949 pitted them against local arch-rivals Halifax. Once again a world record attendance was recorded (95,050), as Bradford took the trophy with a 12-0 victory. Prior to the game the Duke of Edinburgh was introduced to the players. Centre Jack Kitching is seen shaking the Duke's hand. The other players are, from left to right: E. Ward, Leake, Edwards, Davies, D. Ward, Whitcombe, Darlison, Greaves.

Ken Traill, one of the most effective and stylish loose forwards of the post-war period, slings a pass to second-rower Trevor Foster, while Kitching and referee George Phillips watch proceedings. Halifax's South African second rower Jack Pansegrouw prepares to cut off Davies.

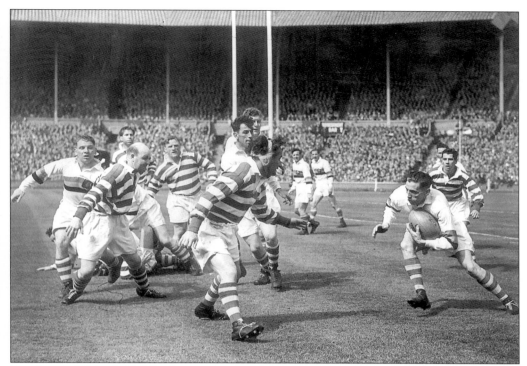

Northern's full-back, Bill Leake, trying to clear his line, braces himself to meet the oncoming Halifax pack. The other Bradford players are Ron Greaves, Trevor Foster, Barry Tyler, Willie Davies and Ernest Ward, who won the Lance Todd Trophy.

Front row forwards Vic Darlison and Frank Whitcombe lift Ernest Ward as the team celebrate their triumph. Bradford's front row laid the foundation for Northern's success by licking Halifax 42-13 in the scrums. From left to right: Dai Rees (manager), Traill, Leake, Tyler, D. Ward, Darlison, E. Ward, Whitcombe, Greaves, Edwards, Davies.

During the triple Wembley years, Bradford Northern came nearest to defeat in the early rounds against St Helens in 1949. On 12 February Saints beat Northern 4-3 at Odsal in the first leg of the first round. Fortunately, the second leg saw Northern scrape through with a 5-0 win at Knowsley Road. Both ties drew crowds of 30,000. The team at St Helens was, from left to right, back row: Tyler, Radford, Greaves, Darlison, Edwards, Traill, Foster. Middle row: Kitching, E. Ward, Carmichael, Batten. Front row: Davies, D. Ward.

Bradford won the Yorkshire Cup five months after the 1949 Wembley success, beating Huddersfield 11-4 at Leeds. An imposing figure in all Bradford's successes of this magical period was second-rower Trevor Foster, pictured striding through Huddersfield centre Jeff Bawden's tackle. Foster certainly ranks amongst the greatest figures in the club's history, having given over sixty years service in a variety of roles. Trevor was regarded by many good judges as the finest forward of the 1940s in both codes of rugby, having played both games at international level during the war.

Ranking alongside the most enduring of all Rugby League's icons, Ernest Ward was Bradford's captain in the glory years of the 1940s. As a centre or full-back he was stylish, artistic and creative. As a leader he was perceptive, decisive and inspirational. He kicked goals too – 538 for Northern in 391 appearances – and also scored the small matter of 117 tries. His career at Odsal stretched from 1936 to 1953 and his impact was such that it propelled him to two Lions tours, in 1946 and 1950, the latter as captain.

Although Bradford slumped dramatically to twenty-first in the league table in 1949/50, Ernest's benefit match still drew a crowd of 10,336 for the visit of Halifax, who beat Ernest's team 7-6. Typically, Ernest scored all Northern's points in the match with three goals.

From 1936 to 1960 Dai Rees, an Australasian tourist in 1924 and a Welsh international back rower with Halifax, was team manager and coach at Odsal. He was a huge influence on playing affairs at the club during the period which brought such prestige to the club and city. This unusual photograph shows him putting forty pairs of boots into store. The boots had been purchased from the departing Kiwi touring team of 1947/48.

Joe Mageen scored 69 tries for Bradford Northern in 202 appearances between 1949 and 1956. Mageen came into the side as the triple Wembley team began to disintegrate, but for three years from 1950 to 1953 he played alongside Ernest Ward in the Bradford centre. At 6ft 1in and over 13st, he was a powerful man who helped solidify the midfield defence. He played in the 1954 and 1956 Roses Matches for Yorkshire, was a member of Bradford's 1952 Championship final team and picked up a winners' medal when Northern beat Hull in the 1953 Yorkshire Cup final.

Action from the 1952 Championship final against Wigan at Leeds Road, Huddersfield. Over 48,000 fans saw Northern go down 6-13 to Wigan – some of them were so keen to obtain a good view that they took to the stand roof! New Zealander Bob Hawes is seen streaking down the wing pursued by Wigan defenders.

Bob Hawes three years later, playing for New Zealand against France. Hawes was one of a colony of New Zealanders who graced Odsal in the early 1950s. A fast and resourceful winger, he scored 69 tries in 99 games for the club between 1950 and 1954, with a best haul of 32 tries in 33 games in 1952/53. Bob claimed the only try of the 1953 Yorkshire Cup final when Hull were beaten 7-2 at Leeds. Bob returned to Britain in 1955 with the touring New Zealanders, playing, appropriately enough, in the Second Test at Odsal.

More action from the 1952 Championship final as Wigan's New Zealand wingman Brian Nordgren is brought to earth by a Bradford tackler. Loose forward Ken Traill (extreme right) is looming over the grounded players while Wigan full-back Martin Ryan (1) moves back on-side.

It is Wigan's turn to defend as their second rower Jack Large topples Northern's skipper Trevor Foster. Northern failed to score any tries in this 6-13 defeat but led 6-5 at one point during the second half.

Jack McLean was probably the most powerful winger who ever played for Bradford and one of the most deadly finishers. McLean was an All Black and also a top-class long jumper, sprinter and decathlete. He joined Bradford in 1950 and terrorised defences for the next six years. His total of 261 tries in 221 games was a club record and almost beggars belief, while his 63 tries in the 1951/52 season has never been beaten. In his last season, 1955/56, he topped the league's try-scorers with 60, including 5 in his final game at Odsal against Swinton.

Another try for Jack McLean as he plunges over against Halifax at Thrum Hall in the Championship semi-final of 1953. Jack scored twice but could not prevent his side losing 16-18. Ron Greaves is the Bradford player on the left backing Jack up. Halifax winger Brian Vierod arrives too late to make any difference.

The Bradford Northern squad of 1951/52. This team finished top of the league but lost to second-placed Wigan in the Championship Final. Huddersfield pipped Northern by one point to win the Yorkshire League and a season which held such high hopes ended trophy-less.

Italy were unusual opponents for Bradford Northern in 1954, as this programme cover portrays. Northern won this fixture 67-18 before a crowd of 7,000, the highest of the seven-match tour. The Italians lost all seven games, including amateur internationals against France and England.

Six
Decline and Resurrection
The 1950s and 1960s

The Bradford Northern team which lost 10-11 at Wakefield Trinity on 10 March 1956. From left to right, back row: Hodgson, Belshaw, Hambling, Glynn, Scroby, Griffett. Front row: Seddon, Smith, McLean, Phillips, Mageen, Oddy, Sutton.

Bill Seddon, Northern's New Zealand centre, races upfield against Featherstone Rovers at Odsal on 5 November 1955. Supporting him is his compatriot Jack McLean with half-back Len Haley in the background. Seddon gave great service to Bradford over eleven seasons from 1952/53 onwards, kicking 304 goals and scoring 45 tries in 284 games.

Another New Zealander, Joe Phillips, takes the ball through supported by hooker Norman Mackie and Jack McLean. Phillips, a wonderfully gifted and attacking full-back (he once scored four tries in a game against Halifax), established a series of club records in his six years with the club between 1950 and 1956. His 1,463 points beat Ernest Ward's old record and his 661 goals remained a record until Keith Mumby broke it in 1983. His 14 goals against Batley in 1952 has still not been exceeded.

A rarity amongst all the New Zealanders was blond South African winger David Knopf, who signed for Bradford in 1953 after trialling at Halifax. In 1953/54, his first season at Odsal, he rattled up 16 tries in 15 games and established himself as first choice right-winger in 1954/55, scoring 10 tries in 37 appearances. Another 4 tries in 5 games in August and September 1955 brought his Odsal career to a close. He then returned to Johannesburg overland via the Sahara Desert.

Bradford knew they had a bargain when they signed Welsh winger Malcolm Davies from Leigh for £750 in 1956. He had scored 79 tries in 84 games for Leigh. By January 1957 he had run in 22 in 19 games for Bradford, including a hat-trick against the Kangaroos. At that point Northern were in the throes of a financial crisis and promptly sold him to Leeds for £3,000, the most they had ever received for a player. Amazingly, by the start of the following season he was back at Odsal, thrilling the fans with 45 tries in 35 games. He left Northern for good in 1959 having piled up 96 tries in 91 matches.

Former Northern loose forward Ken Traill of Halifax goes low on his successor Jack Scroby at Thrum Hall in October 1957. Scroby was another star in the making when he was sold to Halifax in 1959 for a Halifax club record fee of £7,500 as Northern's playing and financial circumstances deteriorated. Jack had played 104 games for Bradford.

The crowd for this cup-tie against Wakefield Trinity, which Bradford lost 3-15, in 1963 was 2,069. Most of the league games at Odsal were actually being played before crowds of only hundreds during this period. Northern's South African second rower Enslin Dlambulo gets his pass away under pressure. Dlambulo scored the last try at Odsal before the 1963 closure.

Another South African forward, Rudi Hasse, is shown the ropes by Bradford chairman Jackie Barritt on arrival at Odsal in 1962.

Bradford's team which lost 9-12 to Batley at Odsal on 12 October 1963, shortly before the club folded. From left to right, back row: Abed, Doran, Hardcastle, Crabtree, Wigglesworth, Gomersal, Hume. Front row: Davies, Reynolds, Haley, Beevers, Carr, Coggle.

Foster shaping new Northern

TREVOR FOSTER

by JACK BENTLEY

THE glorious spirit and history of Bradford Northern Rugby League might yet live on in a new club.

That was the glimmer of hope which came from yesterday's meeting of the League Management Committee who discussed the present set-up's inability to fulfil the fixtures.

BUT . . . before any new organisation could operate the present company, Bradford Northern Football Club Ltd., would have to go into liquidation.

Then the public of Bradford would have to show they wanted senior Rugby League to be played in the city.

Within minutes of the Committee's announcing their decisions one fervent Rugby League supporter, Welshman Trevor Foster. a former Bradford Northern star. had begun a one-man campaign to arouse interest and enthusiasm for a new Northern club.

"I have phoned two business men in the city who have told me in the past they would be prepared to have a go at running a club. Both were out but I intend to contact them as soon as possible." Trevor told me.

"I am convinced that with a good team at Odsal there is a public for the game in Bradford, but you have got to put something in the shop window."

While Foster was brushing up on his "New Northern" plans, Yorkshire county chairman Len Tattersfield was calling a meeting of all Yorkshire clubs for Monday to talk over ways of keeping the club going, and Alderman Revis Barber, chairman of Bradford Corporation's Odsal Stadium sub-committee, announced : "If a new board is formed, I should think the ground will be available to them."

No future

Following yesterday's two-and-a-half - hour management committee meeting in Manchester, League secretary Bill Fallowfield said that when asked if it was a question of wanting the League to " tide them over a temporary financial crisis " Bradford

In December 1963 the unthinkable happened. Bradford Northern ceased to function as a Rugby League club, drowned by debt and unable to fulfil its fixtures. It seemed like the end to many. There was a glimmer of hope, however, if people like Trevor Foster had their way, as this newspaper clipping demonstrates.

Back to the future. On 14 April 1964 a public meeting at St George's Hall paved the way for a revitalised and new Bradford Northern. Around 1,500 people attended and almost £1,000 was pledged to the new club. Joe Phillips can be seen addressing the audience and he went on to become club chairman. Trevor Foster is seated on the platform, hands behind his back.

The new Northern. This is the side which played Huddersfield at Odsal in a first round Yorkshire Cup-tie on 5 September 1964. From left to right, back row: Ashton, Fisher, Rae, Levula, Ackerley, Carr, Lord. Front row: Brooke, Williams, Wilkinson, Abed, Jones, Todd.

- BRADFORD NORTHERN -
RUGBY LEAGUE CLUB (1964) LTD

ODSAL STADIUM · BRADFORD

SEASON 1964-65

GRAND OPENING MATCH
BRADFORD NORTHERN
versus
HULL K. R.
SATURDAY, 22nd AUGUST, 1964
Kick-Off 3 p.m.
Official Programme Price 3d.

The programme for the first match after the reformation of the club in 1964. Hull KR won the game 34-20. The crowd of 13,542 was almost 2,000 more than the total that Northern had drawn to all thirteen of their league fixtures in 1962/63.

By 1965 Bradford were winning trophies again. This group shot from the 1965/66 season contains the players who beat Hunslet 17-8 in the Yorkshire Cup final at Leeds. From left to right, back row: Clawson, Lord, Ashcroft, Hepworth, Williamson, Rae, Ackerley, Hirst. Middle row: Brown, Stockwell, Hardcastle, Smales, Ashton, Morgan, Brooke, Rhodes. Front row: Davies, Walker.

On 21 August 1965 Bradford Northern met the New Zealanders in their second match of the tour and gained a famous 28-15 victory. Terry Clawson scrambles through Graham Kennedy's tackle to score for Northern, backed up by fellow second row forward, Alan Hepworth.

At the other end of the pitch Roger Tait, the Kiwi full-back, evades Northern's South African full-back Mike Brown to score. Dave Stockwell is the other Bradford man in view. Note how much more crowded the Rooley Avenue End is than the Low Moor End in the top photograph.

On Christmas Day 1965 a crowd of 10,059 packed into Thrum Hall to watch Bradford defeat ancient rivals Halifax 15-4. Northern's scrum-half, former Huddersfield and Great Britain captain Tommy Smales, was the match-winner with two tries. Here, he scoots for the posts accompanied by Mr R. Appleyard, the referee.

Ian Brooke and Albert Fearnley were two influential figures in Bradford's revival in the 1960s. Brooke, a world-class centre, played and scored in Northern's first game in 1964 and in the Yorkshire Cup final of 1965. He toured Australasia in 1966. Bradford-born Fearnley became coach in 1966 and for the next decade served the club in various capacities including secretary, general manager and schools development officer.

Queenslander Lionel Williamson joined Northern in 1965 from Halifax, scoring 25 tries in 48 games. He played in the World Cup finals of 1968 and 1970 in which Australia beat France at Sydney and Great Britain at Leeds respectively, scoring two tries in the first and one in the latter. The 'N' on his badge in the portrait does not stand for Northern but for Newtown, his Australian club.

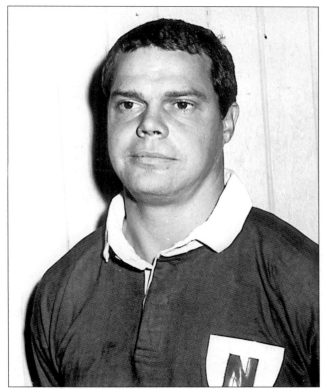

George Ambrum, a burly, thickset Thursday Islander, entertained Odsal crowds throughout the 1967/68 season when he bagged 15 tries in 26 games, including an appearance against the touring Kangaroos. In 1972 he won 2 Australian Test caps against New Zealand. He is pictured giving Halifax winger Terry Michael a hard time in 1967 at Odsal. Scrum-half Bak Diabira is backing George up.

The Bradford Northern squad for the 1967/68 season. From left to right, back row: Taylor, Price, Ramshaw, Clawson, Hill, Kelly, Roberts, Rae. Front row: Fisher, Rhodes, Hepworth, Jones, Kellett, Diabira, Wriglesworth, Stockwell, Ambrum.

Action from Northern's 23-12 victory over Leigh at Odsal on 26 August 1967. Bradford and Leigh were the original pioneers of floodlit Rugby League in the 1950s. Four months after this game, the two clubs again became pioneers as they staged the first games of professional rugby on a Sunday. Northern hosted York while Leigh played Dewsbury on that historic Sunday, 17 December 1967. The Bradford players pictured are Alan Kellett (left), Bob Taylor (11) and Geoff Wriglesworth (3). The Leigh player on the right is a young Jimmy Fiddler, who spent the 1980/81 season with Bradford.

After winning championships with Swinton and Halifax, Ken Roberts signed for Bradford in 1967. A robust, ball-playing prop, Roberts added an air of authority to any pack lucky enough to have his services. Here, he struggles to break free against the Kiwis in a Test at Odsal in 1965. Ken left to play for Rochdale Hornets after making 39 appearances for the club.

It is doubtful if Bradford ever fielded a quicker man than Berwyn Jones, a winger who joined the club for £3,000 from Wakefield Trinity in 1967. Jones was the British and European 100 metres record holder and regarded as the fastest white man in the world when he turned to Rugby League in 1964. His best season for Northern was 1967/68 when he scored 26 tries. He moved to St Helens in 1969 and is seen shaking hands with Saints' great winger, Tom Van Vollenhoven (dark jersey).

Northern built up something of a Welsh colony in the late 1960s. Their biggest capture was undoubtedly Llanelli full-back Terry Price, a player with a howitzer kick, a flair for the unorthodox and a gift for entertaining. Price was a dual Welsh international and toured with the 1966 Rugby Union and 1970 Rugby League Lions. Price played in 123 games from 1967 to 1971 and rattled up 843 points for Bradford before departing to the USA to play American football with the Buffalo Bills.

Hooker Peter Walker makes a midfield break against Hull at Odsal on 17 April 1971. As the '70s dawned Northern were once again scraping along near the foot of the league, finishing fourth from bottom in 1970/71. Walker, in his first season at Odsal, took the Player of the Year award. Remarkably, the following season Bradford shot up to second in the table, Walker being a mainstay of the pack with 34 appearances. Also in view are Peter Small (12), Bak Diabira (7), Stan Fearnley (13) and Graham Wilson (15).

Seven
Promises, Promises
The 1970s and 1980s

Full-back Eddie Tees lands one of four goals in a dramatic 11-7 victory over Wigan at Odsal in the third round of the Challenge Cup on 4 March 1973. Tees set club records of 173 goals and 364 points in 1971/72 which still stand. Tees landed 401 goals for Bradford in only 96 appearances and captained the side at Wembley in 1973.

Action from the Championship quarter-final against Castleford at Odsal on 30 April 1972. Stand-off Mick Blacker avoids a flying tackler and prepares to sidestep Castleford loose forward Cliff Wallis as Northern gain a famous 22-12 victory. Blacker, a versatile, fearless performer, topped 200 appearances for Bradford, scoring 47 tries, and earned a benefit worth a record £4,020 in 1977/78.

Odsal, 4 May 1972. Bradford loose forward Stan Fearnley (13) struggles to shake off St Helens centre Alan Whittle in Northern's first Championship semi-final since 1953. Centre Dave Stockwell, a veteran of 321 games for the club since the reformation in 1964, looks on. Bradford lost 10-14, largely due to a 7-22 flogging in the scrums.

Winger Mike Lamb sails over for a spectacular try against Wigan in the third round Challenge Cup-tie at Odsal in 1973. Northern finished a lowly twenty-third in the league in 1972/73 but went to Wembley with victories over Whitehaven, Hull KR, Wigan and Dewsbury. Unfortunately, in the final Featherstone Rovers comprehensively outplayed them to win 33-14.

The Bradford Northern Wembley squad of 1973. From left to right, back row: Hogan, Earl, Fearnley, Pattinson, Carlton, Long, Gallagher. Middle row: Joyce, Doyle, Cardiss, Dunn, Stockwell, Small. Front row: Diabira, Treasure, Blacker, Tees, Redfearn, Lamb, Seabourne.

**BRADFORD NORTHERN
v BRAMLEY**

Yorkshire Cup -
First Round

Sunday, 31st August 1975   Kick-off 3.30 p.m.   **10p**

In 1974/75 Bradford won the John Player Trophy after beating Widnes 3-2 at Warrington in the final. This is the team which won at Keighley three weeks before the final. From left to right, back row: Jackson, Fearnley, Forsyth, Jarvis, Trotter, Redfearn, Gant, Joyce, Pattinson. Front row: Mumby, Francis, Seabourne, Blacker, Ward, Kelly.

For the 1975/76 season Bradford's match programmes featured a striking bull's-eye cover depicting Stan Fearnley, the team captain, raising the John Player Trophy. Some judicious doctoring of the image must have taken place as the game at Wilderspool had been played in a mudbath. Stan, a veteran of 217 games for Northern, certainly did not finish the game with a lilywhite jersey.

The 1977/78 season saw Bradford Northern lift the Premiership for the first time with a 17-8 triumph over Widnes at Swinton. Skipper Bob Haigh raises the trophy with John Wolford (6) and David Barends (2) savouring the crowd's accolades. Northern reached the Premiership final in the following two seasons only to lose to Leeds and Widnes.

The 1977/78 Premiership winning squad. From left to right, back row: P. Fox (coach), Thompson, Trotter, Forsyth, I. Van Bellen, Roe, N. Fox, Greenwood, Joyce. Middle row: D. Parker, Dyson, Austin, Wolford, Haigh, D. Redfearn, Barends, Mumby, Evans. Front row: A. Redfearn, Harkin, Slater, Raistrick.

Some wonderful pairs of brothers have represented Bradford over the club's long history. Donald and Ernest Ward of the successful '40s side and the present duo of Robbie and Henry Paul are notable examples. Another fine example is the Redfearn brothers. Scoring one of his 241 tries for the club is David Redfearn. A winger capable of running the length of the field, Dave thrilled the Odsal crowds from 1970 to 1988, playing in a massive 435 games for the club. He played in 7 Tests for Great Britain, was a member of the World Cup winning squad in 1972 and toured Australasia in 1974.

Alan Redfearn followed Dave into the Bradford team in 1973 and was Northern's scrum-half for the next decade, making 217 appearances in which he scored 51 tries and dropped 32 goals. Alan was a wily operator at the base of the scrum and an astute link between the backs and the forwards. He was a pivotal figure in Bradford's consecutive Championship wins in 1980 and 1981 and played in successful Premiership, Yorkshire Cup and Players Trophy finals. Alan emulated his brother by touring with the British Lions in 1979 and playing in a Test against Australia.

Ian Van Bellen was a huge prop forward who saw service with several clubs including Huddersfield, Castleford, Fulham – where he was nicknamed 'the Dutchman' – and Halifax. His most successful period, however, was with Bradford Northern, whom he joined in 1977, helping them to win promotion in 1978, the Yorkshire Cup in 1978/79 and the Championship in 1979/80, his final season. Weighing around 18st, Ian often took several defenders with him before parting with the ball and his rumbustious charges took the steam out of opposing packs.

Ian's little brother (only 6ft 4in and 16st), Gary Van Bellen, a powerful, hardworking second rower, signed from Wakefield RUFC in November 1979 and went on to play 202 matches for Bradford over seven seasons. His first two seasons brought him Championship winners' medals. The only final the Van Bellens played together was the 1980 Players Trophy in which Northern beat Widnes 6-0 at Leeds.

The Bradford team of 1978/79 won the Yorkshire Cup and were Premiership finalists. This is the team which routed Rochdale Hornets 30-18 at Odsal on 26 November 1978. From left to right, back row: Fisher, Parker, Gant, Grayshon, Van Bellen, Trotter, Forsyth. Front row: Barends, Stephenson, Fox, Mumby, Redfearn, Harkin.

An auspicious occasion at Odsal on 12 May 1979 as Bradford Northern (dark jerseys) and Widnes show off all the trophies they currently held – they had won everything available between them. Northern held the Yorkshire Cup and the Premiership, although they lost it to Leeds fifteen days later. Widnes held the Championship, the Challenge Cup, the Lancashire Cup, the John Player Trophy and the BBC2 Floodlit Trophy. Widnes won this league game, the last of the season, by 27-19.

Bob Haigh, seen here in Great Britain's garb, had achieved just about everything in the game with Wakefield Trinity and Leeds before he arrived at Odsal in the 1976/77 season. One of the most prolific scoring back rowers the game has seen, he enjoyed an Indian summer at Bradford, leading them to the Premiership in 1977/78.

If ever a player led by example it was prop-forward Jimmy Thompson, a non-stop tackling machine signed from Featherstone in 1977. Ironically, he had been in Rovers' second row when they annihilated Bradford at Wembley in 1973. Jimmy had four seasons at Odsal and was captain of the Championship winning team of 1979/80. He played 145 games for Bradford. Here, he is about to pass the ball in the 1980 Premiership final before Widnes prop Glyn Shaw can tackle him. Jeff Grayshon and Alan Redfearn are the other Bradford players.

Stand-off Nigel Stephenson prepares to unleash second rower Jeff Grayshon in the 1980 Premiership final against Widnes at Swinton. Geoff Clarkson and Dave Redfearn are following up. Stephenson, arguably one of the finest players never to win a Test cap, was one of the most creative players Bradford ever had. He succeeded Thompson as captain in 1980/81 and took Northern to a second successive Championship.

Bradford's successes of the '70s owed as much to the work ethic of some of the team's unsung heroes as to the brilliance of major stars. Amongst those who worked their socks off was second rower Dennis Trotter, whose 201 appearances included 66 off the bench. His long partnership with Graham Joyce gave opposing packs a great deal of grief.

A big favourite at Odsal was the England international prop Colin Forsyth, who came to the club from York for £5,000 in 1974. Forsyth, unstoppable under full steam, had an extraordinary penchant for try-scoring for a prop. In 154 games for Bradford he grabbed 57 tries, including a record 17 in the Premiership winning season of 1977/78. He scored a dozen the following season and 10 in his final season, 1979/80, when he earned a Championship winners' medal.

A colleague of Forsyth at York had been the Bantu winger David Barends, who joined Bradford in 1977. In six years at Odsal he scored 70 tries in 202 games, his best season's haul being 25 in 1978/79. Tremendously strong and determined, Barends made history in 1979 by becoming the first South African to tour Australasia with a Great Britain squad, playing in 2 Ashes Tests. Here, he puts Keighley's defence to the test in 1982.

Coach Peter Fox brought great success to Odsal during his reign from 1977 to 1985, when his teams lifted consecutive Championships in 1979/80 and 1980/81 and also took the Yorkshire Cup, the Premiership and the John Player Trophy. Fox returned to coach Northern between 1991 and 1995 but his teams failed to win any trophies. He is pictured laying down the law to his men at half-time in the game against Leigh on 23 January 1983, which was won 12-9.

Jeff Grayshon takes the ball into the Leigh defence, supported by Gary Van Bellen. Grayshon, most famous as the oldest man to have played top level Rugby League, gave Bradford sterling service from 1978 to 1987, playing 255 games and scoring 37 tries in the process. Grayshon played in 11 Tests while a Bradford player, captaining Great Britain against both France in 1981 and Australia in 1982. His first-class career began with Dewsbury in 1970 and ended with Batley in 1995, when he was forty-six.

Ellery Hanley and Billy Boston, two of the most prolific try-scorers in history, celebrate Hanley's feat of scoring 55 tries in 1984/85. It was the first time any player had passed the 50 mark since Boston had done so in 1961/62. Hanley's professional career began at Bradford, for whom he scored 90 tries in 118 games between 1978 and 1985.

Hanley could also kick goals, landing 83 for Northern. Here, he prepares a shot at goal in a game against Swinton in November 1984. In a game against Hunslet on 7 October 1984 Bradford equalled the club record by winning 72-12. Hanley booted 12 goals and threw in a try for good measure. Hanley was transferred to Wigan in 1985 for a world record fee.

Welsh winger Phil Ford was part of the record deal which took Ellery Hanley from Odsal to Wigan in 1985. In three years with Northern he gave good value, with his elusive running, electric pace and lethal finishing. In 107 games for Northern he scored 59 tries and won 7 Test caps. Perhaps his greatest try was scored in the Third Test at Sydney in 1988 from full-back when he helped Britain to defeat Australia for the first time in ten years.

In December 1985 Bradford Northern made one of the most heralded captures in Rugby League history when they signed Cardiff's Terry Holmes, capped 25 times as a Wales Rugby Union scrum-half, on an £80,000 three-year contract. Already injury prone, he suffered a dislocated shoulder on his debut at Swinton and gave up playing in 1987 after appearing at loose-forward in the drawn Yorkshire Cup final against Castleford at Leeds. A brave but unlucky career at Odsal saw him play only 39 games for the club.

Paul Harkin slings out a pass to John Pendlebury in a game against Hull in 1989 watched by David Hobbs (11) and Brian Noble (9). Harkin, a scrum-half in the old mould – tiny, tricky and with a tremendous kicking game – played as a teenager at Odsal from 1975 to 1979 before moving to Hull KR. He returned to Odsal in 1987. He was the only man to win the White Rose Trophy (man of the match in the Yorkshire Cup final) twice – in 1987 and 1989 – when Northern beat Castleford and Featherstone respectively. He was captain of the 1987 side.

John Woods breaks through the Warrington defence. Woods joined Bradford from Leigh in 1985 for a fee of £65,000. Already capped 10 times in Tests and a proven record-breaker, Woods was effectively the replacement for Ellery Hanley at stand-off. He had to be good and he was – in two years at Odsal, Woods piled up 421 points in only 62 games. On 13 October 1985 he broke Ernest Ward's club record of 34 points by scoring 36 in the form of 5 tries and 8 goals against Swinton, a record which still stands.

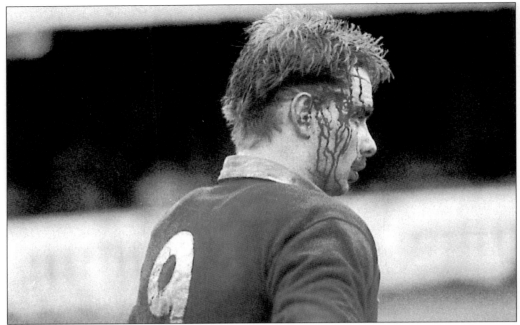

Brian Noble gave blood for Bradford Northern throughout the 1980s and into the early 1990s. A no-nonsense hooker in a time when scrummaging was still a skills area, Noble was another Bradford captain who led by example, always giving of his best, always playing to the last gasp. His industry was rewarded in 1984 when he received the supreme accolade of captaining the British Lions in Australasia. By the time he finished playing he had amassed 392 appearances for the club, which he still serves in a coaching capacity.

Keith Mumby boots the ball to touch at Headingley in the 1982 Yorkshire Cup final against Hull. Mumby has his place indelibly written in Odsal's annals as no Bradford player has played more games (588), landed more goals (779) or scored more points (1,828) for the club. Records apart, Mumby was a paragon as a full-back, totally nerveless under the highest of bombs, deadly in the tackle and adept in attack. His first-team career at Bradford spanned 1973 to 1990, with another short spell in 1993.

Harry Pinner, one of the last of the classic ball-playing loose forwards, shows his colleagues how to deliver a telling pass. Pinner, a former Great Britain Test captain, joined Bradford from St Helens and stayed at Odsal for just the 1988/89 season, playing in 24 games.

Pinner's successor at loose forward was another veteran, John Pendlebury, who was signed from Halifax for a paltry £18,000 in January 1989. He is pictured characteristically getting his pass away under pressure from a Warrington player. Brave, astute and industrious, Pendlebury gave four years of fine service, played in the team which beat Featherstone in the 1989 Yorkshire Cup final and was captain of the side which lost to Warrington in the Regal Trophy final of 1991.

Steve McGowan and Gary Mercer formed a potent centre partnership for Bradford Northern in 1987/88 and 1988/89. McGowan, lanky and long-striding, came to Odsal from Leeds Colts. He played for Northern for a decade between 1984 and 1994, claiming 105 tries in 246 games. Mercer, combative and penetrative, came from Bay of Plenty in New Zealand, for whom he won 20 Test caps from 1986 to 1993. He went on to forge a long career with Warrington, Leeds and Halifax.

Kelvin Skerrett smashes into Warrington's Test loose forward Mike Gregory. Signed from Hunslet in 1987, Skerrett became one of the most formidable props in the modern game, a player opposing fans loved to hate. The international selectors loved him, however. As a Bradford player he won 8 Test caps and a further 8 with Wigan. Skerrett made history in 1990 by moving to Wigan as a free agent, reportedly earning a contract worth £225,000 over three years.

Eight

Bull Mania
The 1990s to the
Millennium Challenge Cup

Robbie Paul hobbles down from the Royal Box at Wembley in 1997, having missed much of the second half with a bad foot injury. Scrum-half Paul skippered Bradford in the 1996, 1997 and 2000 finals. In 1996 he became the first man to score three tries in a Wembley final and won the Lance Todd Trophy – only the sixth player from a losing team to do so in fifty years.

Gerald Cordle bursts down the wing in Great Britain's Test defeat by France at Headingley in 1990. Cordle, a former Cardiff RUFC winger, scored 31 tries for Bradford in 1989/90, his first season in Rugby League. He scored 77 tries in 132 games for the club, playing until 1995 before joining the ill-fated South Wales Rugby League Club.

Bradford Northern trio Karl Fairbank, Deryck Fox and Paul Newlove all played Test match Rugby League in the 1990s. Fairbank's tally of 16 caps is only bettered by one other Bradford player – Ernest Ward, who won 20. Fox won 14 caps but only one while at Odsal – the 1992 World Cup final against Australia at Wembley. Newlove earned 6 caps as a Northern player.

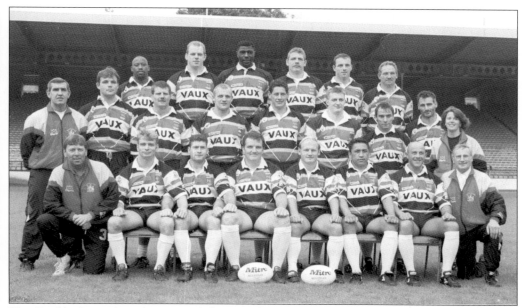

The Bradford squad at the start of the 1993/94 season. From left to right, back row: Roger Simpson, Medley, Powell, Fairbank, Darkes, Mumby. Middle row: Stephenson, Greenwood, Dixon, Hamer, Shelford, Newlove, Holding, McGowan, Marie Griffiths. Front row: John Simpson, Noble, Summers, Hobbs, Fox, Clark, Marchant, Robinson.

David Hobbs tangles with the Workington Town defence in Northern's 28-18 victory in a Challenge Cup-tie at Odsal in 1993. Hobbs, a good leader, a brainy footballer and an excellent kicker, gave sterling service to Bradford from 1987 to 1994. Hobbs's kicking gave him 533 goals in 224 games and won many a game for his team. He landed a century of goals for Bradford in 1988/89, 1989/90 and 1991/92.

Roy Powell was an £80,000 signing from Leeds in 1992, having won 19 Test caps and been a Lion in 1988 and 1990. A tireless, enthusiastic and scrupulously sportsmanlike second rower or prop, Powell made 132 appearances for Bradford before transferring to Featherstone in 1995. When Bradford lost the First Division Championship to Wigan on points difference in 1993/94, Roy had played in all 41 of the club's fixtures. The Rugby League world was stunned when Roy died two days after Christmas in 1998, aged only thirty-three.

The view familiar to all who visited Odsal in the 1990s. The Richard Dunn Sports Centre looms at the top left of the scene. The concreting of the Rooley Avenue embankment in the 1960s somehow served to lessen the dramatic visual impact of the steep old slopes covered in clinker and railway sleepers. The provision of various temporary buildings and retail outlets also tended to hide the vastness of the arena.

In 1996 Bradford reached the Challenge Cup final for the first time in twenty-three years. They scored 32 points but still lost to St Helens who scored 40. The 72 points aggregate was easily the highest ever recorded in a Challenge Cup final, which was hailed by many as one of the best ever seen at Wembley. Here, Paul Medley, the Bulls substitute forward, tries to bump off a Saints tackler.

Graeme Bradley, Bradford's Australian stand-off, is about to fall to a St Helens defender at Wembley in 1996. Bradley had played at Wembley in Castleford's second row when they lost the 1992 Challenge Cup final to Wigan. He would pick up a third losers' medal in 1997 with Bradford.

In 1997 Bradford and St Helens met again in the Challenge Cup final. Saints triumphed once more, 32-22, in a somewhat less frenetic game than 1996. One of the highlights was a super try by Australian centre Danny Peacock, a former Wests, Gold Coast and South Queensland player. Here, he hurtles forward accompanied by winger, Abi Ekoku, who was signed from Halifax a couple of months before the final. Ekoku became chief executive of the Bradford Bulls in 2000.

Bulls' second rower Sonny Nickle seems to be dribbling the ball past St Helens' Chris Joynt as loose forward Steve McNamara looks on from a distance at Wembley in 1997. Nickle, a ferocious and damaging player, arrived with Paul Loughlin and Bernard Dwyer at Odsal in the world record deal which took Paul Newlove to St Helens in 1995. He transferred back to Saints in 1999.

Centre Paul Loughlin brushes off an Auckland Warriors tackler in a World Club Championship game at Odsal in 1997. The tournament was a disaster for English clubs with Bradford no exception to the rule as they lost all six games to Auckland (16-20 and 14-64), Penrith Panthers (16-20 and 14-54) and Cronulla Sharks (10-30 and 12-40). The 1997 season was, however, most successful domestically as Bradford took the Super League title, finishing seven points clear of runners-up London Broncos.

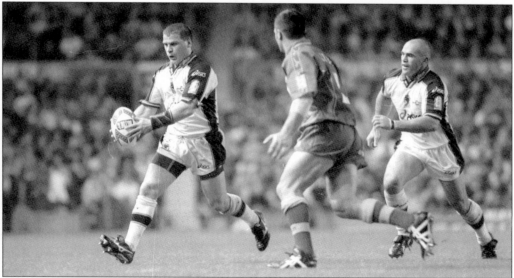

James Lowes moves forward as a St Helens defender approaches during the Bulls' 1999 Grand Final loss to St Helens at Old Trafford. Lowes, a popular figure at Odsal whose strength and determination bring him stacks of tries from play-the-ball situations near the opposing goal-line, has been an unlucky player when it comes to finals. He was in losing teams with Leeds in Challenge Cup finals in 1994 and 1995 and with Bradford in 1997 and in Leeds's Premiership final defeat by Wigan in 1995. Murrayfield 2000 was worth waiting for, however.

Edinburgh's famous Rugby Union stadium, Murrayfield, was the scene of the 2000 Challenge Cup final. It was the first time that a cup final had been staged away from Lancashire, Yorkshire or Wembley and Bradford were the stars of this historic occasion, beating Leeds 24-18. Two early tries from Michael Withers set up the victory. For the first he profited from a steepling bomb from Henry Paul to fly over at the corner with Iestyn Harris unable to challenge.

Withers scores his second try after only sixteen minutes, again from a tantalising up-and-under from Henry Paul. Leeds winger Leroy Rivett (18) is too late to stop the touchdown. Rivett, the previous year's Lance Todd Trophy winner, completely misjudged both of Paul's kicks to allow Withers a dream final.

Winger Nathan McAvoy scores the third Bradford try after 28 minutes to give his team a 14-2 lead. McAvoy's try was a delightful cameo as he burst down the flank and delicately chip-kicked past Harris, collected the ball in flight without breaking stride and scored without being touched.

Prop Paul Anderson, the biggest man on the Murrayfield pitch, raises the plinth of the Challenge Cup. Anderson overcame a long history of injuries and illness to become a potent weapon in the Bulls' armoury, often playing in short spells in which his full power would devastate opposing sides.

At last, the cup goes back to Bradford. Skipper Robbie Paul holds the 103-year-old trophy aloft alongside his brother Henry, winner of the Lance Todd Trophy. Bradford had not won the Challenge Cup for fifty-one years. The drought finally ended on 29 April 2000 on a field which had been submerged under 3ft of water 48 hours earlier.

The Bulls celebrate their tartan triumph. At the extreme left stands eighteen-year-old Leon Pryce with his hand on Bernard Dwyer's shoulder. The two men had appeared as substitutes. Pryce had waited just over a season to claim a cup winners' medal. Dwyer, aged thirty-three, had played in four previous finals (two with St Helens and two with Bradford) and lost them all.